de

Corbières and Minervois: tree-lined lanes snaking through
vineyards and scrubland, Romanesque abbeys and Cathar castles
perched on hill-tops…

Left page

Majestic Carcassonne… ten centuries of history look down from the heights of its walls.

… the Mediterranean coastline: miniscule harbours, seaside resorts and above all lakes and marshes, a strange, amphibious land where man has celebrated the union of land and sea for thousands of years. The Montagne Noire (Black Mountains): powerful scenery of breathtaking gorges, weather-beaten mountain tops, lakes with red- and ochre-coloured banks and mediaeval villages. Finally Carcassonne, splendid and proud, a dream in stone untouched by the passing centuries. Aude is more than just a *département*, it is a universe in miniature, containing some of the most dazzling scenery and architecture in France.

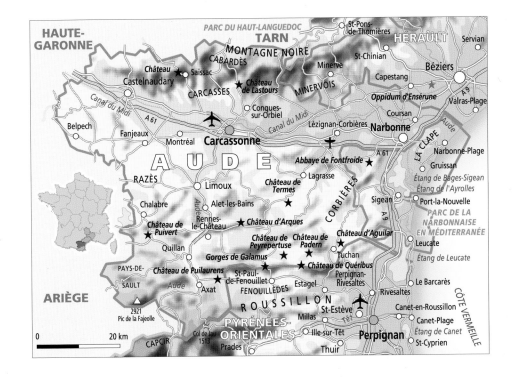

ALET-LES-BAINS

It is hard to believe that this peaceful little town, nestling in the shelter of a green valley, has had such a long and eventful history. In fact, the town has been a thermal spa since Roman times, when the curative powers of its hot springs were already well-renowned. A large Benedictine abbey was established here during Carolingian times and it became a cathedral town at the beginning of the 14th century. The Wars of Religion were fatal to both the cathedral – which was razed to the ground in 1577 – and the abbey, of which only ruins remain. In contrast, the mediaeval village, with its narrow streets lined with half-timbered houses, has retained all of its character.

BAGES AND SIGEAN

On a promontory overlooking a lake measuring almost 5,500 hectares that was once the gulf of Narbonne before being cut off from the sea, Bages invites walkers to discover steep alleyways interspersed with stairways, the ramparts and a charming little fishing harbour. South of the lake and now located over a mile from its banks, Sigean was once the entry port to Corbières. There is an Italian feel to its narrow streets. The church of the Penitents, with its wrought-iron dome and the *musée des Corbières*, with its displays of archaeology, ornithology and popular traditions alone are worth a look. Nearby, the 250-ha African reserve at Sigean has hundreds of animals in semi-liberty – including rhinoceros, elephants and ostriches.

Above
An Italian atmosphere pervades the alleyways
of Sigean…

Top, left
The 250-ha African reserve at Sigean has hundreds
of animals in semi-liberty – including lions,
rhinoceros and elephants.

Left
The village of Bages, overlooking
the calm waters of its lake.

CARCASSONNE

There are just under two miles of ramparts forming two concentric enclosures, fifty-two towers, drawbridges, barbicans, battlements, ditches and moats, gates so heavily fortified that one of them, porte Narbonnaise, could pass for a fortified castle. The old walled town of Carcassonne is still the largest fortress in Europe and a unique example of mediaeval military architecture. It is true that the restoration project mooted by the writer Prosper Mérimée and carried out between 1844 and 1870 by the architect and restoration expert Eugène Viollet-le-Duc contains some errors and approximations. As it appears today, however, the town is quite a good representation of its "probable former state" – in the words of Viollet-le-Duc – of a fortified town in the Middle Ages.

Traditionally, visitors to the town enter via porte Narbonnaise, which is flanked by two 13th-century towers and preceded by a drawbridge. Just past the gate are the Lices, an immense parapet walk stretching between the two enclosures. Then, via the steep, narrow rue Cros-Mayrevieille – whose picturesque cobblestones and old houses give it a picturesque quality that not even the innumerable souvenir shops can obliterate completely – you reach the castle, built in the 12th century by the Trencavel family, viscounts of Carcassonne. It was from this "fortress within a fortress", protected by moats, thick ramparts and six towers, that the lords of the town coordinated the defence in the event of a siege. The basilica of Saint-Nazaire-et-Saint-Celse, with Romanesque nave, Gothic chevet and transept, and 13th- and 14th century stained-glass windows, is a veritable architectural treasure. Apart from these three major buildings, visitors should visit the towers which are open to the public (including those of the Narbonnaise, the Vade, the Tréseau and the Inquisition gates), stroll around the alleyways of the town and walk the length of the magnificent Lices parapet walk between the two enclosures.

The *bastide* town of Saint-Louis, too often overlooked by visitors, was built in the 13th century at the foot

Left
The entrance to the
castle and bridge.

of the town on the banks of the river Aude and is well worth a visit. With its characteristic grid pattern and handsome old houses, the complex is charming, and the 14th-century *pont Vieux*, 13th-century cathedral of Saint-Michel and Carmelite chapel are worth more than a flying visit.

Top of page
The Bastille Day fireworks display attracts tens of thousands of spectators to Carcassonne on July 14th.
© P. Cartier.

Below
When visitors go through the porte d'Aude, which leads to the duke's castle, they become aware of how powerful the town's fortifications are.

CASTELNAUDARY AND THE ABBEY OF SAINT-PAPOUL

The name alone immediately evokes cassoulet, for which it claims paternity, along with Toulouse and Carcassonne. But the capital of Lauragais has many other assets than this wonderful dish. Pierre-Paul Riquet turned it into the main port of the canal du Midi between Toulouse and Lake Thau, after which it enjoyed over two hundred years of prosperity. Today, thanks to the popularity of water-based tourism, Castelnaudary has revived its past as a port. The 7-hectare Grand Bassin (main pool), where in bygone days you would find dozens of horse-drawn barges and small boats berthed, is now full of life again, at least during the summer. The old town, with its alleyways lined with old houses and classical-style mansions, is worth a lengthy visit. The major monuments include the collegiate church of Saint-Michel, a handsome example of southern Gothic architecture, whose bell tower bizarrely straddles a street; the Présidial, which was the town's *castellum* and was demolished in 1355 by the Black Prince, before being rebuilt for use as a courthouse and prison; the

Top of page

The cloister in the abbey of Saint-Papoul.

Left

The Grand Bassin, or main pool, of Castelnaudary, the largest port on the canal du Midi.

chapel of Notre-Dame-de-la-Pitié, which has 18th-century gilded panelling; the *hôpital Saint-Jacques*, whose apothecary contains a rich collection of china and porcelain; and finally, the *moulin de Cugarel*, the last of the town's thirty-two mills, which occupies a position with panoramic views.

The abbey of Saint-Papoul lies a few miles from Castelnaudary. It was founded by Charlemagne in the 8th century and was a bishop's seat from 1317 to the Revolution in 1789. The cathedral, with 12th-century chancel and 14th-century nave, is notable for its exterior sculpted capitals, the work of Maître de Cabestany, an anonymous 12th-century sculptor. With its episcopal palace and 14th-century cloister, with arcades decorated with vegetation and monstrous figures from the Romanesque bestiary, the abbey of Saint-Papoul is a little-known treasure, like the village itself, which, with its ramparts and typical mediaeval timber-framed houses, has a peaceful charm in perfect harmony with its abbey.

Right
The site of the *moulin de Cugarel* offers wonderful views over the Lauragais plain.

FONTFROIDE

The beauty of the site, a small valley lost in the rocky hills of Corbières, is matched only by that of the sandstone abbey, which is seen – deservedly – as one of the prettiest in the South of France. Founded by the Benedictines in the 11th century, the abbey went on to adopt the austere Cistercian rule. Fontfroide was at the heart of the fight against the Cathars and was highly influential throughout the Middle Ages, to the extent that one of its abbots was even elected pope. It has been in private ownership since the beginning of the 20th century and has been immaculately restored. The abbey church, the 12th-century cloister, the main courtyard, the monks'- dormitory and refectory, the Louis XIV courtyard and the rose garden all combine to make this a wonderful place.

Right page
The rose garden at the foot of the abbey church.

Left
The Gothic cloister is considered one of the most beautiful in southern France.

Below
In a harsh landscape of scrubland and *maquis*, the abbey of Fontfroide appears like a miracle…

Wonderful

Languedoc-Roussillon

Text **René Gast**

Photography **Jacques Debru**

Translation **id2m**

Editions OUEST-FRANCE

Summary

Aude • 5

Gard • 31

Hérault • 53

Lozère • 97

Pyrénées-Orientales • 121

The main festivals in Languedoc-Roussillon • 140

The Royal Canal and quays of la Marine in Sète.

GRUISSAN

Separated from the sea by the still water of the lakes, this mediaeval village, with its burnt ochre tiles, crowns the rocky promontory where the ruins of *château Barberousse* (Redbeard's castle) stand guard. The circular streets, façades and burnt ochre rooftops of the fishermen's and wine growers' houses lend it a powerfully original character. There are 1,300 wooden huts on stilts, on the huge beach lined up in staggered rows. This strange place was the inspiration for Jean-Jacques Beineix when he was making his film *Betty Blue*. This may compensate in part for the disappointing architecture of Port-Gruissan marina, built near the village in the 1960s.

Below
The beach at Gruissan is renowned for windsurfing.

Above
The ruins of château Barberousse still watch over Gruissan.

LA CLAPE

To the north of Gruissan, between the plain of Narbonne and the sea, an astonishing rocky limestone range suddenly appears. La Clape – meaning the pebble – with its gorges, cliffs, pits, lakes and hills covered with vines and pine trees and its scrubland filled with the scent of thyme, myrtle and rosemary, is a little world of its own, so well protected that rare plants, such as *Centaurea acaulis*, have been able to survive here. In this walkers' paradise there are waymarked footpaths and, for the motorist, a few winding roads, linking the main centres of interest of this range, including the hermitage of Notre-Dame-des-Auzils and its marine cemetery, the *gouffre de l'Oeil-Doux* – a spectacular 100m-diameter depression containing a salt lake – the villages of Fleury, Saint-Pierre-sur-Mer and Armissan, the hamlet of Cabanes-de-Fleury on le Grau de Vendres and, finally, Hospitalet, which has many attractions for the visitor, including a vineyard and several museums with eclectic collections ranging from old cars to fossils.

Above
The hermitage of Notre-Dame-des-Auzils.

Left
The pit of l'Œil-Doux, linked to the sea by underground channels.

LAGRASSE

This pink-roofed village nestled on the banks of the river Orbieu and surrounded by hills covered in vines and scrubland is simply delightful. The village's mediaeval alleyways are lined with timber-framed houses, the ruins of ramparts (*porte de l'Eau, tour de Plaisance*), a superb covered marketplace dating from 1315, a souvenir of the markets which made it its fortune in the Middle Ages, when it was the capital of Corbières, and a 12th-century bridge – *pont Vieux* – over the Orbieu.

But it is the abbey, above all, that makes Lagrasse one of the most beau-tiful sites in the Aude region. Founded in the 8th century, it had enormous spiritual and political influence up until the Hundred Years' War. After three centuries of decline, it underwent a brief revival in the 18th century, before being sold off as a national heritage property at the time of the Revolution. Like Font-froide, it is now privately owned. From the outside, visitors are struck by the size of a 40m-high bell tower/keep, which offers wonderful panoramic views. Next, visitors can visit the classical-style abbatial palace, the 12th-century cloister, the 13th-century church, the 10th-century Pre-Romanesque tower – the oldest part of the abbey – the monastic buildings, which include an enormous dormitory in the shape of an upturned hull, the old two-storey Romanesque cloister and finally the Abbey chapel, which has polished paving and wonderfully crafted frescoes.

Above
The daring elegance of the pont Vieux, which crosses the Orbieu at the entry to Lagrasse.

LIMOUX

This town is known chiefly for its *blanquette* – a sparkling white wine "invented" at least four centuries before champagne. It is also known for its carnival which, since the 14th century, takes place every Sunday during January and on Ash Wednesday. What many people don't know is that Limoux has kept some lovely souvenirs of its prosperous past as a centre of the textile industry. These include a 13th-century tower, a testament to the power of the mediaeval ramparts; the Romanesque-Gothic church of Saint-Martin, which houses a 15th-century silver and gilt reliquary among other treasures; the Augustinian convent with its 14th-century façade; the old quarter, with its superb old aristocratic houses hidden among a maze of alleyways – *rue Toulzane* and *rue de la Blanquerie*, for example; the half-timbered houses and arcades in *place de la République* and *pont Neuf,* built over the Aude in the 14th century to link both parts of the town. Visitors should also stop off at Catharama (47 rue Fabre-d'Eglantine), which has an audiovisual display retracing the history of the Cathars.

Above
The covered arcades in *place de la République*.

Below
Women who don sumptuous, poetic costumes for the carnival are known as *Los Femnos.*

NARBONNE

This was one of the most beautiful – perhaps even the most beautiful – towns in Roman Gaul. Ideally placed at the bottom of what was once a deep gulf, this town was a busy port and major centre of trade between Marseille and Spain. Up until the end of the Roman Empire, it was the capital of an immense province – la Narbonnaise – that stretched from the Pyrenees to the Garonne and the Rhône. The Great Invasions could have sounded the town's death knell had the Visigoths not in turn declared it their capital. Thus, the town only started to decline in the 14th century, when the gulf became choked with sand, a consequence of the Hundred Years' War and the ravages of the Black Death.

Paradoxically, very little remains of the town's glorious Gallo-Roman past. Deprived of its seaport, the town was effectively turned into a stronghold in the 16th century and stones were taken from the Roman monuments to build the ramparts. The only piece from this period to survive is the Horreum (the granary), an atmospheric labyrinth of cellars, decorated here

Above
The place de l'Hôtel-de-Ville, dominated by the Palais Neuf, the keep of Gilles-Aycelin and the tower of Saint-Martial.

Below
The basilica of Saint-Just-et-Saint-Pasteur: southern Gothic at its peak.

and there with sculptures and bas-reliefs, and which no doubt was used as a warehouse. The Middle Ages, however, left many architectural traces, the most spectacular of which is the monumental ensemble of the Archbishops' Palace and the basilica of Saint-Just-et-Saint-Pasteur.

The former is divided into two distinct buildings, separated by the *passage de l'Ancre*. The first building, the 12th-century *Palais Vieux*, has two wings surrounding the keep of *la Madeleine*. The façade of the second, the 14th-century *Palais Neuf*, was restored by Viollet-le-Duc and is flanked by the keep of Gilles-Aycelin and the tower of Saint-Martial. Apart from the Town Hall, the *Palais Neuf* houses the *Musée archéologique* and the *Musée d'Art et d'Histoire*. The basilica, with its two enormous bell towers and graceful flying buttresses, is considered one of the most beautiful Gothic buildings in the South of France. Although unfinished – the

nave was never built – it is nevertheless an imposing structure, with the height under the chancel arches at 41m. At its foot, the 14th-century cloister and the Archbishops' garden complete the harmonious architectural picture. No trip to Narbonne would be complete without a walk along the quays of the *canal de la Robine* and a visit to the quarter of Saint-Paul, with its old houses – including the justly famous *maison des Trois-Nourrices* – and the Romanesque-Gothic basilica of Saint-Paul-Serge.

Above
In the heart of Narbonne, the canal de la Robine winds its way just under the houses…

Right
Via Mercaderia, a reconstruction of the court of love of Viscountess Ermengarde (12th century).

NATURAL REGIONAL PARK OF NARBONNAISE EN MEDITERRANEE

This recently opened park extends over 80,000 hectares of highly diverse landscapes, including limestone cliffs and lagoon-like lakes, dry scrubland and wetlands. The highly diverse climate conditions – mainly Mediterranean and mountainous – support a wide variety of biotopes. With no fewer than fifty different types of natural environments, it is rich in fauna and flora, containing almost 2,000 higher plant species and 300 species of birds, many of them migratory, that – like in the Camargue region – find here a favourable environment to stop over or over-winter. However, the originality of the natural sites, such as La Clape (see p. 15) and the island of Sainte-Lucie (see p. 22) are not the only attractions of the park: villages such as Bages and Sigean (see p. 6), with their perfectly preserved architecture, are among the finest in the Aude.

Above
The canal de la Robine and its towpath, shaded by umbrella pines.

Below
A path through scrubland near Port Leucate.

Above
Corbières vines and the chapel of
Saint-Félix, near Castelmaure.

Above, right
Vineyards around Fontfroide

Right
A *capitelle* – wine-maker's shelter – near
Fitou.

The park: a few figures

The park features 80,000 hectares, a population of 36,500, 20 miles of Mediterranean coastline, 8,000 hectares of wetland, 300 hectares of beaches and dunes, 20,000 hectares of sea, 740 hectares of salt marshes, 24,000 hectares of scrubland, 6,500 hectares of forests, 15,000 hectares of vines, and has 15,236 hectares of sites scheduled for inclusion in the Natura 2000 network. ■

PORT-LA-NOUVELLE

While Port-la-Nouvelle – the third largest French Mediterranean port – is not strictly speaking a tourist destination, the surrounding area harbours some real treasures. To reach it, take the strange and poetic *route des Étangs* from Bages. This uncertain region where the land and sea meet, an inextricable mix of marshland, islands and lakes, where people have made a living from fishing, vineyards and salt since time immemorial, is still home to the pink flamingo, the egret, bulrushes and reeds. The *Sentier botanique* on the island of Sainte-Lucie, between lake and sea, and the *Sentier cathare* that passes through the scrubland to the charming village of Lapalme, are not to be missed.

Finally, to the south of Port-la-Nouvelle, you could stop off at Leucate. The fortress, built on a promontory, gives a lovely panoramic view of the village, lakes and Corbières. On the coast, the cliffs at cap *Leucate* offer some lovely paths for walkers and cyclists. Finally, between the old village and the seaside resort of Port-Leucate, there are miles of fine sandy beaches.

Above
The lake of Leucate, where holiday-makers now outnumber fishermen and salt workers.

Below, right
On a quay in Port-la-Nouvelle…

Below, left
The peaceful paradise of the island of Sainte-Lucie.

RENNES-LE-CHÂTEAU

You would need a good deal of imagination to believe that this modest village was a royal city at the time of the Visigoths. It had formidable ramparts and was large enough for over 30,000 inhabitants. But troops from Aragon, followed by Simon de Montfort's crusades, destroyed almost six glorious centuries of history. Visitors don't come to Rennes-le-Château today for its past, of which little remains, nor for its superb location, but rather to dream of the unresolved mystery of an immense treasure believed to have been discovered here at the end of the 19th century by Abbé Saunière, the parish priest. After years of secret digs, the priest suddenly became rich, restoring the church at great expense, buying up land and building a villa, a tower, an orange grove and a huge park. Many theories have been advanced to explain this mystery - that the treasure found by Abbé Saunière belonged to the Visigoths, the Cathars, the Knights Templar or Blanche of Castile. Or perhaps it was the Holy Grail or the Ark of the Covenant … The fact remains that practitioners of the occult, diviners and treasure seekers have been coming to Rennes-le-Château for decades, in the hope of getting their hands on what remains of the mysterious priest's loot – even though digs are forbidden.

Below
The tower of Magdala, a look-out post on the path to hidden treasure.

Below
Was it the devil that tempted Abbé Saunière?

CATHAR CASTLES
IN THE AUDE REGION

Catharism – from the Greek *katharos*, which means "pure" – and the terrible repression suffered by its adherents have made an indelible mark on the memory of Southwest France. There is hardly a town or village which does not bear the scar of the massacres, pillaging and destruction that accompanied the crusades mounted by the Church with the support of the kings of France, who saw in them an opportunity to annex rich territories. The Cathar doctrine, which came from the East, is based on the principle of the fight between Good, which is desired by God, and Evil, the work of Satan. Man's soul belongs to Good and his body belongs to Evil. Thus, in order to attain the kingdom of Good, man must take a vow of poverty, chastity, humility and labour, fast regularly and keep to a vegetarian diet, abstaining from killing any life, even that of an animal. The Church could not remain indifferent to a doctrine which rejected certain sacraments and which criticised its wealth and the loose moral standards of its clergy. In 1208, using the murder of one of his legates as a pretext, Pope Innocent III launched the first crusade against the

Below
Perched 400m high over the plain of Tuchan, Aguilar closed off access to central Corbières.

Peyrepertuse
This town's nickname is "Celestial Carcassonne". Words fail to do justice to the fabulous fortress, the largest of all the Cathar fortresses: perched over the abyss, it resembles a town more than a castle, with 1 1/2 miles of ramparts, two castles, a church and houses, dominated by the keep. ■

Aguilar
Perched on a 400m-high hill dominating the neighbouring plain, Aguilar is protected by two many-sided enclosures, round towers and a keep. Like Termes, it fell to Simon de Montfort in 1210. ■

Above
Peyrepertuse owes its reputation as
an almost impregnable fortress to
Saint-Louis, who reinforced its defensive
system.

Right
Having lost all strategic usefulness after
the treaty of the Pyrenees, Puilaurens
was used as a prison for a time.

Puilaurens

Along with Aguilar, Peyrepertuse,
Quéribus and Termes, this enormous
castle, on a 700m-high summit, with its
ramparts and large keep, was one of
the "five sons of Carcassonne", sentries which stood guard on the Aragon
border. Reputedly impregnable, it finally fell to the crusaders in 1256. ■

Puivert

Even though Simon de Montfort took it without much difficulty, Puivert's fate was not as tragic as that of many other Cathar castles. Once peace returned, it housed a famous "lovers' court" for many years, where the real lords were troubadours. Its 35m-high, 14th-century keep, houses a chapel and three rooms, one of which is called the Musicians' Room, with ribbed vaulting decorated with sculptures. ■

Termes

This fortress, like an eagle's nest, surrounded by ravines and protected by a double enclosure, was long considered impregnable. However, after a four-month siege in 1210 by Simon de Montfort, its exhausted defenders were compelled to surrender through thirst and dysentery. The crusaders' success here considerably weakened Cathar resistance. ■

Above

The taking of Puivert was a disappointment for the crusaders, as all its defenders had escaped through tunnels…

Right

Raymond, lord of Termes, one of the great Cathar chiefs, was captured here, and later died in prison.

Above

The fall of Quéribus followed closely on from that of Montségur and signalled the definitive victory of the crusaders.

Quéribus

It was here that the Cathar heresy came to an end in 1255, at least on the military front. Perched atop a 728m-high rocky peak and dominating an extraordinary landscape of arid mountains, this "citadel on the precipice", its walls merging into the rock face and its many-sided keep housing a superb Gothic room, is one of the most beautiful examples of mediaeval military architecture. ■

Below
The château de Padern was
one of the last bastions
of Cathar resistance.

Above
Saissac, perched on a rocky
ledge surrounded by ravines.

Below
The remains of Cabaret and
Tour Régine, two of the four
castles in Lastours.

Albigensians, as they were also known. Knights from the North, who had been promised the same spoils as for a crusade to the Holy Land, and who dreamt of carving out fiefdoms in the rich countries of the South, rallied to the call. Led initially by Simon de Montfort up until his death in 1218, the incredibly cruel crusade was then led by his son, Amaury. Cathar strongholds fell one after the other but the heresy was far from being wiped out when Louis VIII, King of France, launched a second crusade following a call in 1226 from Pope Honorius III. To make it more efficient, Pope Gregory IX set up the Holy Inquisition in 1233, whose courts were charged with tracking down and judging heretics. In spite of this deployment of means, the Cathars resisted for another thirty years. It was only in 1255, after the fall of Quéribus, their last stronghold, that they were defeated, at least on the military front, as their religion continued to be practised in secret.

The heroic ruins of the Cathar castles, around which resistance to the crusades was organised, stand on the highest peaks of Corbières. As sublime and austere as the "Good Men" and "Perfects" who defended them, Termes, Aguilar, Quéribus, Peyrepertuse and Puivert stand as a permanent reminder, not only of one of the worst crimes ever perpetrated by Christians against Christians in the name of the same God, but also of the death of one of the most brilliant civilisations in mediaeval Europe.

Above
The keep of Arques, built in the 13th century by Gilles de Voisin, a lieutenant of Simon de Montfort.

Gard

Take a large portion of the Camargue, a slice of the Mediterranean and a piece
of the Cévennes. Sprinkle with scrubland, vineyards, forests, torrents, lakes,
beaches and mediaeval villages…

Left page

The Pont du Gard, a colossal
masterpiece, two thousand years old,
and still almost entirely intact…

… Decorate with Roman monuments and towns as old as civilisation, season with thyme and lavender, and then heat under the sun of the South. Hey presto, you get le Gard, a *département* of inimitable flavours, where the wilderness lives in surprising harmony with highly civilised landscapes and dazzling architectural treasures.

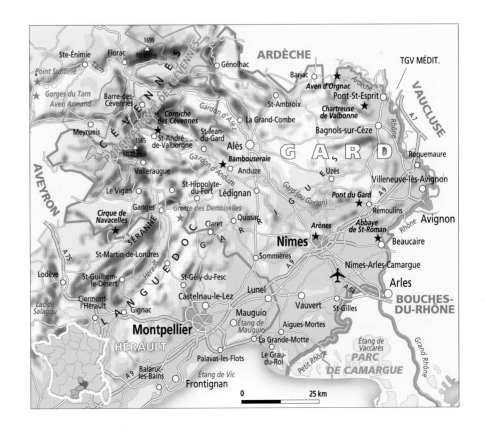

AIGUES-MORTES

The great 18th-century writer Chateaubriand once described this place as "a great ship run aground". Looming like an apparition along the horizon of salt marshes and swamps, Aigues-Mortes, located in an amphibious, unworldly place where previously only impoverished fishermen dared venture, was built by Saint Louis as an embarkation point for his crusades to the Holy Land. With its geometric layout, its crenellated ramparts, towers and fortified gates, the old town is an admirably well-preserved model of mediaeval military architecture. Its decline, which began in the 15th century, was not due to recurrent plague and cholera epidemics nor to the Hundred Years' War. It was, rather, the progressive silting-up of the channel linking it to the sea, followed by the building of Sète harbour that dealt Aigues-Mortes the final blow. However, its beauty has remained intact over the centuries and tourism is now offering salvation.

Above and below

Every year in August, the Saint-Louis festival serves as a reminder that Aigues-Mortes was the starting point for the 7th crusade.

Camelles (piles of salt) on the Salins du Midi site.

ALÈS

Say the name and you will immediately think of Emile Zola's novel *Germinal*, with its mine shafts, firedamp explosions, coal tips and the destitution of the working classes. However, all this is but a dim and distant memory. The centre of Alès today is charming and the cathedral of Saint-Jean, the *fort Vauban*, the town hall and some lovely houses are well worth a look. The town has not, however, forgotten its mining past, as the fascinating museum of industrial archaeology, the *Mine Témoin d'Alès*, will attest, with its 600m of underground galleries containing reconstructions of the miners' working methods and conditions in bygone days.

Right
The cathedral of Saint-Jean-Baptiste d'Alès.

Above
Aigues-Mortes, a port until the coast silted up, stands guard over an amphibious world of swamp and salt marshes.

ANDUZE

Visitors will love this little town, located as it is at the end of a transverse valley, dominated by high cliffs. They will also love the charm of its alleyways and fountain-filled squares and pottery workshops that keep alive the ancient tradition of Anduze vases. They will love it because it is an ideal base for discovering the Cévennes. A little over a mile from the town, the 10ha bamboo plantations of Prafrance hold one-hundred-and-fifty species of bamboo, some of which are higher than 20m. It would be a pity to miss this amazing place.

Below
The two thousand-year-old art of its potters has made Anduze famous.

Above
The bamboo plantations of Prafrance.

BEAUCAIRE

This town seems to have come straight
out of a time when towns were built
for people, with bright and shady
streets, secret houses, cheerful, flower-
filled quays and the castle, whose
proud ruins continue to watch over a
sea of pink rooftops. Although no
longer that wealthy town, whose annual fair – the biggest in 18th-century
France – attracted over 300,000 people, each of its stones seems to hold
the memory of its former prosperity.
Before going to see the main monuments, such as the *château royal,*
with its 14th-century triangular high
tower and enclosure, the 18th-century
collegiate church of Notre-Dame-des-
Pommiers and the 17th-century town
hall, stroll through the streets and
squares lined with handsome houses
– place Vieille, place Clemenceau and
rue de la République, to name a few –
and along the quays of the Rhône and
the canal, to get a taste of the peaceful
charm of a near-perfect town.

Above
Although dismantled in 1632 on
the orders of Cardinal Richelieu, château
de Beaucaire has lost none of its austere
splendour.

Left
Yachts have replaced barges on the
quays of Beaucaire

Above

Cormorants and pink flamingos…
The lakes of Camargue remain one
of the richest bird reserves in Europe.

LA CAMARGUE GARDOISE

Immense areas of swamp, rice fields and flooded grassland stretching to the horizon, pink flamingos flying overhead, galloping horses, immobile ebony-coated bulls… this is Petite Camargue, 20,000ha of lowlands, where the Rhône and the sea stretch from the south of Nîmes to the Petit Rhône to the east and to the *canal du Rhône* in Sète to the west. On old offshore bars you can find isolated *mas* and a few, rare, pink-roofed villages, such as Vauvert, Montcalm and Gallician. But the main interest of a visit to Petite Camargue lies in its flora and fauna; its lakes, Scamandre, Charnier and Grey; its swamps, including the huge Souteyranne, its *sansouïres*, intermediate areas between swamp and lake and its rice fields and salt marshes.

Because of bulls, quicksand in marshland areas and the rarity of walkways – the whole area is almost entirely occupied by private properties closed off with barbed wire – it is difficult to discover Petite Camargue properly on foot. However, the area can be discovered by canoe or kayak or by hiring a houseboat to sail down the *canal du Rhône* from Sète. Visitors can also get a good idea of the fauna and flora of the Camargue by taking a walk around the *Centre de découverte de Scamandre*, a 220-ha natural reserve, or by contacting one of the few guides available for walking, horse-riding or 4x4 tours. Further information can be obtained from the Tourist Information Centres of Aigues-Mortes, Grau-du-Roi or Vauvert.

La source Perrier

This is a fascinating visit for industrial tourism enthusiasts. Just over 4 miles from Vauvert, near Vergèze, is the Perrier spring. A guided tour allows visitors to follow the course of the famous bubbly drink, from the source at Bouillens to bottling. ■

Le Grau-du-Roi

Located on the coast of the Petite Camargue, this fishing port gets its name from the Occitan word *grau*, which means a natural canal between a lake and the sea. While the old village has retained much of its charm – its quays are home to a large fleet of trawlers – Le Grau-du-Roi is famous today mostly for the neighbouring resort of Port-Camargue, an immense marina which, with nearly 4,500 berths, is Europe's foremost marina. ■

Above
The castle at the Perrier plant.

Right
Camargue horses and cattle egrets.

Below
The fishermen return to Grau-du-Roi.

NÎMES

This is a lovely town, both lively and peaceful, where the shady alleyways, gardens, quays and squares filled with flowers and parasols invite you to linger a while. The ancient town of *Nemausus*, situated on the via Domitia, the trade route to Spain, was one of the most beautiful and refined towns of Roman Gaul. In the Middle Ages, Nîmes alternated decline with prosperity, before becoming an important centre during the 16th-century Reformation. The Protestant middle classes, rich from banking and the textile industry, turned Nîmes into the "French Rome" in the 18th century. Its intellectual and artistic influence extended well beyond the borders of Languedoc.

With such a past, Nîmes could well have become a museum-town and rest on its architectural laurels, but it hasn't. The town has maintained its ancient, mediaeval and classical monuments but has also had the audacity to commission prestigious architects and contemporary designers to add to the town's monuments. The results are sometimes debated but never leave indifferent. Finally, it has got rid of the Sleeping Beauty image that it once had: its three annual ferias – the Winter festival in February, the Pentecost festival in June and the Wine Harvest festival on the third weekend in September – attract crowds from all over France.

Above
Detail of the fountain of Martial Raysse.

Below
Bullfighting remains popular in Nîmes; for proof, look at the crowds in the arenas during the féria…

Maison Carrée, built circa 5 A.D., is one of the best-preserved
Roman temples in the world.

Above
The Tour Magne was once part
of the town walls.

There is not enough space here to
list all the treasures Nîmes has to offer. The arenas were inherited from
the Romans, built on the model of the
Colosseum in Rome, and they are reputed to be the best preserved in the
world. It also inherited the *Maison
Carrée*, a temple dedicated to Caius
and Lucius Caesar, the *porte d'Auguste*
and the Castellum, a vestige of the
aqueduct across the pont du Gard.

The most striking remnant from the Middle Ages is the *tour Magne*, a souvenir of the town's fortifications, and the Romanesque frieze that decorates the façade of the cathedral of Notre-Dame-et-Saint-Castor. Many Renaissance- and classical-style houses can be discovered by taking a walk around the historic centre, through *place du Marché, place aux Herbes, place des Esclafidous, rue de l'Aspic, rue Dorée, rue Fresque* and *rue du Chapitre.* Next, you shouldn't miss the *jardins de la Fontaine,* which are steeped in the spirit of the Age of Enlightenment. They were the first public gardens in France. Modern architecture lovers will enjoy a visit to the *Carré d'Art* by Norman Foster, the council housing estates by Jean Nouvel, the bus shelters by Philippe Starck, the *place d'Assas* revisited by Martial Raysse and the *Musée des Beaux-Arts*, the town hall and the marketplace, all redesigned by Jean-Michel Wilmotte.

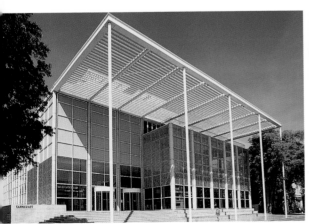

The *féria* of Nîmes

The Pentecost *féria* in Nîmes, the largest in France, attracts almost one million people every year, making it one of Europe's most popular festivals. While the bullfighting is the main draw – Nîmes rivals those temples of bullfighting, Seville or Toledo – it has much more to offer. Over three days and three nights, the town takes on a supercharged atmosphere, as it throws itself into Spanish-style celebrations, with flamenco, salsa and penas, while in the *bodegas*, fino sherry, pastis and *costières de Nîmes* flow, accompanied by dozens of tapenades and tapas. This huge, spontaneous and larger-than-life, both religious and pagan festival, is one of the few remaining genuinely authentic French festivals. ■

Top left

"Abrivado"… The horse, like the bull, remains a Camargue passion.

Bottom left

The *Carré d'Art* houses a multimedia library and a museum of contemporary art. The *jardins de la Fontaine* were laid out in the 18th century on part of the site of the old Gallo-Roman town.

Opposite

During the *feria*, Nîmes becomes even more Spanish than usual.

PONT-SAINT-ESPRIT

For a long time, its sheer breadth, power and unpredictability made the Rhone very difficult to cross. Fords where merchants in ancient times and the Middle Ages could transfer their goods from one bank to another without risk of loss were few and far between, and bridges were even rarer. In the mid-10th century, the abbey of Cluny built a Benedictine monastery near Saint-Saturnin-du-Port, a small fishing village located at a much-used crossing point. The priors of the monastery took the initiative to build the bridge that was to give its name to the town. This was a colossal enterprise: the bridge, built using ancient techniques, is almost 919 metres long and took forty-six years (1265-1309) to finish. Up until the Revolution, it was maintained by the order and funded by a salt tax, known as *petit blanc*. The order also built a chapel and two hospices, one for abandoned children, the other for sick pilgrims, on the bridgehead. A major staging post on the road to Santiago de Compostela, the town made its fortune from taxes on goods transiting between Provence and Languedoc. This is evident in the rich architectural heritage: 18th-century town houses, fountains, the church of Saint-Saturnin (14th and 15th centuries), the 17th-century chapel of les Pénitents-Bleus, the 18th-century chapel of the Visitation, the priory of Saint-Pierre, the citadel and collegiate church all make up an astonishing ensemble of religious and military architecture that mixes Gothic and classical styles – not to mention the bridge itself, whose twenty-five arches have spanned the Rhone for over seven hundred years.

Left page
The quai de Luynes, on the right bank of the Rhone.

Below
This double-flight staircase is framed by the churches of Saint-Pierre on the left and Saint-Saturnin on the right.

THE *PONT DU GARD*

This triple-tiered bridge has 64 arches. It is 275m long, 48m high and has 21,000m³ of stonework laid without the use of mortar. Some of the stones weigh 6 tons and the total weight is over 50,000 tons. The figures are impressive, but fail to convey the shock felt when discovering this incredible wonder for the first time. The *Pont du Gard* is the most spectacular remains of a thirty-one-mile-long aqueduct which supplied Nîmes with 400 litres of drinking water per second, a technical achievement that seems all the more incredible when you learn that the average slope from the source is only 0.34m/km. The crossing of the Gardon had made it necessary to build this bridge. Building commenced in 1 BC and took only five years to complete, in spite of its colossal dimensions. Although poorly maintained after the fall of the Roman Empire, it was in use until the 11th century, a thousand years later, before being

Opposite
The Tour de l'Horloge,
in Vers-Pont-du-Gard.

Below
The Pont du Gard, generally considered the eighth wonder of the world.

converted into a bridge during the Middle Ages, which was used by vehicles until the 19th century. Up until its final years, its approaches were invaded by anarchic car parks and fairground stalls, an insult to the masterpiece which attracted almost two million visitors. Since the year 2000, the site has been rehabilitated, with well-hidden buildings housing a multimedia museum, a café and shops. The car parks have been moved away and discovery pathways opened up. On summer evenings, James Turrell's spectacular multi-coloured light show adds a fairytale touch to the regained nobility of the eighth wonder of the world.

Near the *Pont du Gard*, visitors should not miss out on some of the prettiest villages in the region. These include Vers-Pont-du-Gard, which, apart from the charm of its streets and flower-filled squares, has some remarkable old wash-houses, and Castillon-du-Gard, with its mediaeval houses and the Romanesque chapel of Saint-Caprais, Saint-Hilaire-d'Ozilhan and the 11th-century chapel of Saint-Etienne.

Top of page
Cobblestone street and mediaeval houses in Castillon-du-Gard.

Right
The preserved grace of
La Roque-sur-Cèze and its houses
on the hill.

SAINT-GILLES

You'd need a lot of imagination to convince yourself that in the Middle Ages this quiet backwater was an embarkation point for crusaders off to the Holy Land, one of the most visited places of pilgrimage in Europe and a major staging post on the road to Santiago de Compostela. From this illustrious past, Saint-Gilles has retained an old town with superb Romanesque and Renaissance residences, including the *Maison romane*, where Pope Clement IV was born, and the 12th-century abbey-church of Saint-Gilles. The purity of its lines, the beauty of the Romanesque sculptures on its façade and its extraordinary *vis de Saint-Gilles* – a staircase with a unique helical structure – make it one of the masterpieces of religious architecture in Languedoc.

Above
The sublime simplicity of the façade of the abbatial palace of Saint-Gilles.

SAINT-ROMAN

There are two reasons to stop off at Saint-Roman. The first is that it is the only troglodyte abbey in Europe, built into the rock face from the 5th century onwards. The second is the magnificent panorama over the Rhône valley from the open necropolis at its summit.

Left
The abbey was built entirely into the rock during the 5th century and is the only one of its kind in Europe. It contains cells and rooms for collective use, such as a refectory, a chapter house and a chapel. A necropolis was hollowed out of the rock nearby.

SOMMIÈRES

"I must admit that I have never seen anything as pretty as Sommières". How could you not approve Lawrence Durrell's accolade of the town where he ended his days? In a Tuscan landscape of hills and vineyards stand the ruins of a mediaeval castle, cobbled streets, tiny squares lined with arcades, splendid houses hidden behind modest, narrow façades... And then there are the *pétanque* players, playing in the shade of plane trees and the *belote* players in the shady corners of cafés... "Sommières is a lot of fun; it is profoundly marked by the spirit of actors Fernandel and Raimu" added Lawrence Durrell. Stroll down *rue de la Taillade* and *rue Bombe-Cul*, walk along the quays of the Vidourle, stop before the *tour de l'Horloge* and its belfry, wonder at how the Roman bridge has managed to remain in such good repair after twenty centuries of loyal service, then, after a rest under the cool arcades in *place des Docteurs-Dax* or *place Jean-Jaurès*, climb up to the castle via *montée des Régordanes* and to get a vast panoramic view of the town's rooftops, the Cévennes and the peak of Saint-Loup...

Above

The castle of Villevieille, built in the 11th century and restored during the Renaissance. It was one of Saint-Louis and then Louis XIII residences. It is said that Mirabeau saved it from destruction during the French Revolution.

Right

The quays of la Vidourle and Sommières keep, built on the site of a Gallic oppidum. During the Roman period, the town was a major military and trading crossroads.

UZÈS

When you see its high towers braced as if to challenge the elements, you will realise that Uzès is not a town like any other. It's hardly a town at all, just a little backwater of 8,000 inhabitants. But what a past! What a heritage! Founded in ancient times – perhaps by the Greeks in the 6th century BC – in turn a Roman *castrum*, a bishopric from 419, then elevated to the rank of duchy in 1565, the town has a longer history than most French towns. After long-lasting prosperity between the 16th and 18th centuries, due mostly to the textile industry, the town started to decline and turn to ruin. It was writer André Malraux who resurrected the town during the 1960s, when it had become a forgotten backwater between Nîmes and Avignon. Now magnificently restored, the "premier duchy of France" has been returned to its former glory.

Above

The Tour Fenestrelle, arcades and a house on the place aux Herbes: the architectural heritage of Uzès is exceptionally rich.

The pearl of Uzès is the *Duché*, a group of buildings formed by the *Château des Ducs*, which has a Renaissance façade, the 15th-century Gothic chapel, the *tour Bermonde* and an 11th-century keep, and which has been in the private ownership of the Crussol d'Uzès family for ten centuries. Other major monuments include the *tour Fenestrelle* – one of a kind, its round tower and 42m-high window considered one of the pure masterpieces of Romanesque art – which stands elegantly beside the 18th-century episcopal palace and the cathedral of Saint-Théodorit, whose 19th-century façade is a little disappointing perhaps, but which houses a very beautiful 17th-century organ with a painted case. While wandering around the town – which must be done on foot – you will discover many old houses and luxurious mansions – including that of the baron of Castile, near the cathedral – particularly around the *place aux Herbes*, with its mediaeval houses which were "modernised" in the 17th century and have now been magnificently restored. Dally awhile on the romantic *promenade des Marronniers*, where the house after which it is named stands as a reminder of playwright Jean Racine's long stay in Uzès.

Right
The *Foire à l'Ail* or garlic fair in Uzès takes place on the fourth Thursday of July in place aux Herbes.

THE CHARTERHOUSE OF VALBONNE

This ancient walled monastery stands in the middle of a spectacular forest. Founded in 1204 by Guilhem de Vénéjan, bishop of Uzès, it was severely damaged during the Wars of Religion, was rebuilt in the 17th century and then abandoned after the Revolution. It was restored during the 19th century by Carthusian monks. The monks left in 1901 and, twenty-five years later, the charterhouse was turned into a clinic for tropical diseases. Nowadays, it houses a hotel, conference rooms, a renowned vineyard and a sheltered workshop, fulfilling both a social and tourist function. The colourful herring-bone pattern of the roofs of the monastic buildings is strangely reminiscent of the architecture of Burgundy. The fortified enclosure, the church (17th-18th centuries), with its remarkable vault and 19th-century inlaid stalls, the faithfully restored small cloister, all make up a complex of rare harmony.

Below
Between vineyards and forests, the long-abandoned charterhouse has found a new lease of life…

VILLENEUVE-LÈS-AVIGNON

The overbearing proximity of the City of the Popes – separated only by the river Rhône – could have totally eclipsed this town. However, Villeneuve is not a suburb of Avignon but a town in its own right, with superb monuments and a history just as long as that of its better-known rival. Villeneuve was a strategic site for the kings of France – the other bank of the river was part of the Roman Empire before becoming home to the popes – and it remained a stronghold throughout the Middle Ages, an affirmation of royal power facing that of the Holy See. This did not prevent many cardinals and at least one pope, Innocent VI, from choosing to live here. Places to see include the f*ort Saint-André*, whose formidable ramparts surround the town like an acropolis, the 14th-century Charterhouse of Val de Bénédiction, located in the centre of the old town, the tower of Philippe le Bel, a keep built in 1307 to secure access to the pont Saint-Bénézet – the famous pont d'Avignon – the 14th-century collegiate church of Notre-Dame and, finally, the *Musée Pierre-de-Luxembourg*, located in a 14th-century palace which was rebuilt in the 17th century, and which houses some masterpieces of mediaeval art.

Right
The tower of Philippe-le-Bel (above) and the roofs of the old town, huddled around the collegiate church of Notre-Dame.

Hérault

It smacks almost of favouritism… the *Constituants*, members of the French Revolutionary Assembly, who drew the borders of Hérault, seem to have wanted to include all the best landscapes of the South of France here.

Left page

The untouched wilderness of the cirque de Mourèze…

The splendid ruggedness of the foothills of the Massif central, the alternating violence and calm of the hills of Minervois, the wide horizons on the Languedoc plain quivering with vines and fruit trees, the lagoons and sands of the Mediterranean… not to mention its towns, so beautiful and each so different: Montpellier, bubbling and cultured, Béziers, with its almost rural wisdom, Sète, which looks like a ship setting sail. A land of contrasts? Yes! It might be a cliché, but for Hérault, as for no other *département*, it is true.

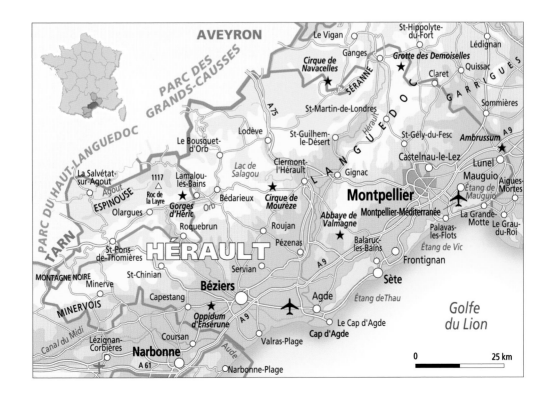

AGDE

The Phoenicians who founded this town twenty-five centuries ago called it "Agatha", which means beautiful. Conquered by the Visigoths and then by the Arabs, it was destroyed by Charles Martel who believed it would put a stop to the Muslim advance. The town next came under the control of the Trencavel family, lords of Carcassonne, and then under that of the bishops at the end of the 12th century. Before being pushed back inland by a coastal embankment, Agde was one of the richest ports in the western Mediterranean over a long period. However, the building of Aigues-Mortes by Saint Louis, followed by that of Sète under Louis XIV, meant that its importance steadily declined, despite the Canal du Midi being routed through here, for which Riquet built a round lock that remains one of his masterpieces. It is as if the town, "the black pearl of the Languedoc", was in mourning for its former glory, built as it is into the ash-coloured volcanic rock. The austere mass of the cathedral of Saint-Etienne, with its thick walls, bell tower-keep and battlements, looks more like a fortified castle than a religious building. The façades of the town hall and the old houses that line the streets and squares of the old town are made of dark basalt … Agde is clothed in a black, volcanic stone which could be seen as sinister, were it not for the sun of the South, illuminating the façades and gables, even into the most secret passages. In its unpredictable streets, on joyous quays where rickety houses are reflected in the Hérault river, everything breathes gracefulness.

Above
The "black pearl of Languedoc", which here, however, looks pink and golden on the banks of the Hérault river.

Left
The cathedral of Saint-Étienne, fortress of the faith.

Above
The plage Richelieu at Cap-d'Agde, and, in the distance, the island of Bresou and its fort Vauban.

Right
The plage de la Grande-Conque at Cap-d'Agde.

Cap-d'Agde

Handsome cliffs, black basalt beaches, a huge modern seaside resort and Europe's most popular nudist colony… This tiny volcanic **Brescou** island off cap d'Agde has an interesting 16th-century fort, which was redesigned in the 17th century by Marshal Vauban and used as a state prison for many years. ■

Ephebe of Agde
Discovered at the bottom of the Hérault river in 1964, this Hellenistic bronze statue (dating from the 2nd century BC) is a splendid testament to the Greek origins of the town. You can see it at *Musée de l'Éphèbe*, in Cap-d'Agde. ■

AMBRUSSUM

Located 21/2 miles north of Lunel, this ancient *oppidum* or town, fortified in the 4th century B.C, is perched on a hill that has probably been inhabited since the Stone Ages. In the late 1st century B.C. on the eve of the *pax romana*, Ambrussum abandoned its defensive position to become one of the many staging posts along the 300-mile long Via Domitia (see p. XXX). The remains, which are open to the public, retrace a 5,000-year-long history and their extensiveness is astonishing given that Ambrussum was little more than a modest backwater during the Roman empire. The most spectacular ruin is without contest the pont Ambroix, where the Via Domitia crosses the Vidourle river. Once 100 metres long, only one of the eleven original arches still stands. The reason for this is that the local people started to dismantle the bridge at the end of the Middle Ages and flash floods to which the river was subject destroyed many arches, the last of them in 1933. About 200 metres of the roadway itself have remained more or less intact. Along the way, forming the lower town, are amenities similar to those found in motorway service areas today: inns, an area for horses and carriages, baths, a forge for vehicular repairs and a church – early versions of today's secular motels, car parks, restrooms, a garage and a chapel. On the site of the ancient *oppidum* – the upper town – visitors can still trace the route through streets laid out in the original grid pattern. The houses lining these streets, the largest of which measured over 4,300 square feet, housed huge numbers of slaves in addition to their owners. There was once a paved square with a large public building, the purpose of which remains unclear. The square was surrounded by a rampart that was 635 metres long and contained twenty-six towers and which is still visible today.

Left page
At the foot of the old town or *oppidum*, the paving stones of the Via Domitia bear the scars of over twenty centuries of use.

Below
This arch on the pont Saint-Ambroix is the only one to have withstood the flood waters of the Vidourle.

BÉZIERS

Béziers is without a doubt quieter than Montpellier and less magical than Carcassonne. But it is such a beautiful town – the sight of the high silhouette of the cathedral, beyond the arches of the *pont Vieux* reflected in the Orb river, dominating the acropolis, never fails to take your breath away – it has such a gentle way of life – notwithstanding the violent, southern passion for rugby, bullfighting and wine (!) – that it is always a pleasure to spend time here. It has, however, a stormy, often bloody, history. During the crusade against the Albigensians, for example, when the Catholics refused to hand over the Cathars, the crusaders embarked on a terrible massacre, to the cry of "Kill them all, God will recognise his own", issued in all Christian charity by the papal legate. In spite of sieges,

Top of page
Saint-Nazaire Cathedral, view of the cloister.

Left
Between Béziers and bullfighting, an age-old love story…

Below
The Jean Moulin memorial on the Plateau des Poètes.

pillages and fires, the town has retained many architectural treasures. Walk around the streets of the old town and discover fine mansions in, for example, *rue du 4-Septembre* or *rue Mairan*, the superbly restored *halles Baltard*, two Romanesque churches, Saint-Jacques and la Madeleine – in the latter, in 1209, thousands of women, children and old people had their throats cut – and finally the Gothic chapel of les Pénitents-Bleus. Overlooking the town and the Orb valley, the cathedral of Saint-Nazaire

was built between the 12th and 15th centuries on the site of a church burnt down by the Crusaders. From its amazingly restrained Gothic cloister, you can access the charming secret Bishops' garden, which has exceptional views over the rooftops, the 12th-century *pont Vieux* and the river Orb. Other interesting sights outside the old quarters include the basilica of Saint-Aphrodise (10th-century nave, 14th-century chancel), the romantic *jardin du plateau des Poètes* and the "ladder" of Fonsérannes, one

of the most astonishing works of art on the *canal du Midi*. Just like in Biterrois, you can finish the day at one of the café terraces in Pierre-Paul Riquet's alleyways, those *ramblas* shaded with plane trees, which are the real heart of the town.

Above

The Orb river, the Pont Vieux and the cathedral of Saint-Nazaire dominate the old town.

Resurrection of a wine-making region

Béziers' long history is inextricably linked to wine – the Greeks are credited with introducing vines to the region over 2,500 years ago. Wine-making in Béziers reached its height in the 19th century, when the railway boom allowed local wine-makers to export their produce throughout France and beyond, as far afield as Italy and the Baltic countries. Wine merchants and large-scale wine-makers made huge fortunes and built grandiose castles, known as *châteaux pinardiers*, while Béziers was embellished with sumptuous gardens, mansions and other buildings. However, the ravages of the Phylloxera epidemic, followed by the fraudulent practice of adulterating wine carried out by unscrupulous wine-makers and competition from Algerian wine, led to long-lasting decline. Throughout most of the 20th century, the reputation of Languedoc wines almost never rose above the mediocre. Over the last two or three decades, however, wine-makers have mounted a spectacular fight-back, ripping up vines, improving plant selection and wine-making technology, drastically changing the image of the region's wines. According to experts, some Languedoc *appellations d'origine contrôlées* – Corbières, Fitou or Minervois among others – now rank among the finest of French wines. ■

Above

The Italianate theatre, with its façade by the sculptor David of Angers, forms the northern boundary of allée Paul-Riquet, the *ramblas* of Béziers.

Right page

Gayonne is one of the *châteaux pinardiers*, grandiose castles built by rich wine merchants in the 19th century. It is now home to the Béziers Academy of music.

CLERMONT-L'HÉRAULT

With its back to the mountains and facing the plain, this very ancient town, founded by the Phocaeans about 700 years BC, owes its prosperity to wine and olives. The remains of its ramparts – there are seven towers still standing – and its feudal castle remind the visitor that during the Middle Ages this was a stronghold of major importance. The old town, with its steep streets dotted with stairways and multi-denominational houses, has retained its mediaeval feel and one of the region's most beautiful Gothic buildings, the collegiate church of Saint-Paul (12th-14th centuries), can be found here.

Above
The harvest of *lucques*, olives renowned for their delicate flavour.

Below
The feudal castle of Clermont-l'Hérault: mediaeval military architecture in all its brutal efficiency…

Around Clermont-l'Hérault

A couple of miles from Clermont is the *Manufacture royale* in Villeneuvette, built around 1670 and developed with the support of statesman Jean-Baptiste Colbert, which produced wool cloth until 1954. If you visit the perfectly restored buildings, you will understand what daily life was like for the weavers over the course of three centuries.

Near the delightful village that gave it its name, the *cirque de Mourèze*, 5 miles from Clermont, is an amazing 300-ha mass of rocks, covered in waymarked footpaths. This is a sight not to be missed…

The man-made lake of Salagou (3 miles from Clermont) occupies the site of an ancient crater. Its red sandstone banks form a strange and magnificent backdrop. ■

Bottom, right
The oppidum at Ensérune and,
below, the dried up lake of Montady.

ENSÉRUNE

Languedoc has several sites identified as oppidums, pre-Roman and Gallo-Roman fortified towns which gave shelter to the local population for centuries. The oppidum of Ensérune, built on a 100-m high rocky ledge overlooking the Biterrois plain, is the most remarkable. Archaeological digs have uncovered well-kept remains of fortifications, house foundations, silos, pottery and money from successive civilisations over the course of seven or eight hundred years: Iberian, Greek, Gaul and Roman. In all likelihood destroyed several times, including once in the 3rd century BC by Hannibal, the oppidum grew to prosperity after the Romans came, to the point where its population grew to 8,000 inhabitants under Augustus. But from the middle of the 1st century AD, the town became progressively deserted, as the *pax romana* induced the population of Narbonnaise to abandon its defensive sites.

Above, right
The lake of Salagou
and Notre-Dame-des-Clans.

Above, left
Old weavers' houses
in Villeneuvette.

LAKE THAU

Separated from the Mediterranean by a thin 12-mile long strip of land, at 8,000ha, Lake Thau is the largest on the Languedoc coast. More than a lake, it is a veritable small inland sea, with beaches, resorts and harbours (Balaruc, Bouzigues, Marseillan, Mèze), fishing fleet, fishermen and even storms. Since ancient times, a major source of income for the inhabitants of its banks has been shellfish farming. As far back as Roman times, people have loved the flat Belon oysters that proliferate in the wild. Sadly, the fragility of the environment has meant the disappearance of indigenous oysters. The oysters sold today under the name *bouzigues* are oysters from highly

Left

Oyster beds in Lake Thau... in contrast to Marennes or Belon oysters, "Bouzigues" oysters are permanently submerged in suspended tray cultures.

The open-air Noilly Prat wine and spirit store.

Noilly Prat wine and spirit store in Marseillan

It's a strange sight, hundreds of barrels lined up in a huge courtyard. The famous vermouth, made according to a secret recipe using light white wine and around twenty different plants, is left to age in oak barrels in the open air, exposed to the elements. The store is closed in January and February. ■

resistant Japanese stock which is just as tasty. They are farmed using a technique adapted to the absence of tides: in suspended culture trays where the oysters are permanently submerged, reaching maturity at between 12 and 20 months, a year less than for Atlantic and English Channel oysters. The small towns around the lake are charming. Balaruc-le-Vieux still has its ramparts, from which there is a beautiful view of the lake, and it also has a fortified church dating from the 14th century. The following are all worth a visit: Mèze, with its remains of fortifications, Loupian, with its fortified gates, its arcaded streets and 4th-century Roman villa, Bouzigues, with its shellfish trays and *Musée de l'Étang de Thau*, and finally Marseillan, its lively fishing harbour, black basalt houses, its church of Saint-Jean-Baptiste and its famous distillery.

Above
Bouzigues, the oyster-farming capital of Lake Thau.

Below
The church of Notre-Dame-de-la-Conversion and its bell tower/keep.

FRONTIGNAN

Already famous during Roman times for the quality of its wines, this large winemaking town has retained its title as the capital of Muscat wine for over twenty centuries. Frontignan was also a port, the largest in Languedoc in the 17th century. Its Mediterranean character, museum, devoted in large part to wine – naturally – 12th-century fortified church of Conversion-de-Saint-Paul, which has a door decorated with boats and fish, echoing the town's fishing past, and the *plage des Aresquiers* all make it a pleasant place to stop.

LA GRANDE-MOTTE

Love it or hate it... the gigantic pyramid-shape buildings, designed by architect Jean Balladur, leave nobody indifferent. La Grande-Motte is today the symbol of urbanisation on the Languedoc coast powered by the State in the 1960s to respond to the demands of mass tourism. A triumph of avant-garde architecture or the irreparable disfiguration of an exceptional maritime landscape? It's up to you to judge…

Top of page
The marina of La Grande-Motte: a controversial style of architecture that has, however, garnered a widespread following…

Left
The plage de La Grande-Motte.

LODÈVE

To the south lie the Languedoc plain and its vines, to the north the Larzac plateau and its sheep. Wedged between these two different worlds lies a small town that has been Gaulish, Roman and Visigoth and the seat of a powerful bishopric for twelve centuries. Lodève originally prospered thanks to the wool industry before turning to uranium mining. Although the castle which overlooks the town from the top of Montbrun is nothing but a ruin, and the ancient quarters have retained only a hint of the past, Lodève has an exceptional building: the cathedral of Saint-Fulcran, remarkable for the height of its tower (57m) and its fortifications, is one of the masterpieces of southern Gothic architecture.

Le Larzac

Lodève is the starting point for a visit of Larzac, the southern part of which belongs to Hérault. Visitors will remember the time when locals fought against the extension of a military camp here. And when you see the splendour of the landscape of this immense limestone plateau or *causse*, when you see the fierce beauty of fortified farms and villages, a good example being Le Caylar, 12 miles from Lodève, you will understand why the watchword *gardarem lou Larzac* was followed with such determination. ■

Right
The cathedral of Saint-Fulcran in Lodève.

Below
Larzac plateau, where one of the most famous French peasant uprisings took place.

MINERVE AND MINERVOIS

Balanced on a rocky ledge, perched above the gorges of la Cesse and le Brian, it's not surprising that the "town on the precipice" was named after a goddess: it is simply divine. Behind the shelter of natural fortifications – canyons, cliffs and escarpments – and man-made ramparts, Minerve was one of the most powerful Cathar fortresses. In 1210, the town capitulated before the troops of Simon de Montfort and a hundred and eighty Cathars were burnt alive by the Inquisition. The old town, overlooked by *La Candela*, the remains of a mediaeval castle tower, has retained its exceptional character. The old parapet walk, which overlooks the Brian canyon, is a good way to walk around the town. There are many interesting buildings to see here, including the *porte Basse*, the *porte des Templiers*, the *tour de la Prison* (Prison tower), the well of Saint-Rustique, the "Malvoisine" catapult – which bombarded the town with killer blocks of stone during the siege of 1210 – and above all

the 11th-century Romanesque church of Saint-Etienne, which houses a white marble altar dating from the 6th century, one of the oldest in Europe. Near the town, a short walk brings you to the natural bridges of limestone rock that cross the river Cesse.

Minerve is the capital of a "land" of powerful originality. Between vines and scrubland, olive groves and forests, a tour, which includes several incursions into Aude, opens up a number of unforgettable sites, including La Caunette, a fortified village with a very beautiful 13th-century gate and a charming Romanesque church; Rieux-Minervois, which has a 16th-century castle, rampart remains and ancient houses and a famous Romanesque church of unusual design, based on the figure 7, which is unique in Languedoc; Caunes-Minervois, known for its marble quarries – the most spectacular of which are Notre-Dame-du-Cros – and its Romanesque abbey-church Saint-Pierre-et-Saint-Paul. Take a spin down the country roads and stop off at the caves of La Coquille (3 miles from Minerve) and Bize (just over a mile from Bize-Minervois), at the village of Aigne, with its original spiral layout, and, near Cesseras and Ciran, at the *dolmen des Fades* and the chapels of Saint-Germain and Notre-Dame-de-Centeilles.

Top
Chancel of the Romanesque church of Rieux-Minervois.

Above
Minerve, heart of the Cathar resistance
and one of the martyred towns.

Below
A Muscat vineyard near
Saint-Jean-du-Minervois.

Above
The chevet of the abbatial palace
of Saint-Pierre-et-Saint-Paul
in Caunes-Minervois.

Above
Fête des Associations in Antigone.

Below
In the heart of the old town, place
Jean-Jaurès is one of the most lively
and cheerful in Montpellier.

MONTPELLIER

Montpellier has had a curious destiny. The indisputable capital of Languedoc-Roussillon, rich, industrious, young and lively – students make up a quarter of its population – compared to its neighbours, it is a relatively new town, as it was founded just a thousand years ago! Founded in the 10th century when two villages were joined, the new town developed rapidly with maritime trade – its outer port, Lattes, was very active at this time. It became a major staging post on the pilgrimage to Santiago de Compostela and to the Holy Land and was home to a university of great repute throughout Europe, where the great writer Rabelais came to study

medicine. After the torment of the end of the Middle Ages and the Renaissance – the epidemics, the Hundred Years' War and the Wars of Religion – the town regained its prosperity in the 17th century thanks to wine growing and the chemical and textile industries.

There are two sides to Montpellier, which is both aware of its past and forward-looking. The modern, perhaps even resolutely avant-garde side, has new quarters, such as Antigone, designed by Ricardo Bofill, audacious, sometimes controversial buildings, such as *Le Corum*, which is both a convention centre and an opera house, and daring new projects, such as the construction of Port-

Marianne, which will provide a link to the sea. The other side is that of the old town, which has been almost entirely pedestrianised. It has retained its mediaeval layout, which is of such architectural wealth that it would be futile to attempt to describe it all.

Although located just outside the historic centre, the *place de la Comédie*, designed in the 18th century, is the true heart of the city. The most remarkable monument here is the theatre, redesigned by the architect Garnier. The streets and squares in the old town – *rue de la Loge, rue des Trésoriers-de-la-Bourse, rue de l'Argentine, rue de l'Ancien-Courrier, place Saint-Ravy…* the list goes on

Above, left
This recently restored triumphal arch marks the main entrance to the historic centre, also called *L'Ecusson*.

Above, right
The cathedral of Saint-Pierre and its astonishing fortified door.

Above
The 'Flower Waltz' (choreographed by Dominique Bagouet) at the festival of dance in Montpellier.

Below
Since reopening in February 2007, the Fabre museum has been hugely popular.

The Fabre museum
Closed for four years for structural improvements, the Fabre museum in Montpellier reopened its doors to the public in February 2007. Now completely refurbished, it has over 99,000 square feet of exhibition space, with some 900 works from the 15th to 21st centuries, organised by theme and chronology. Boasting Flemish and Dutch collections, 18th-century collections, paintings by Delacroix, Géricault, Courbet, Corot, the great impressionists, 20th-century painters – Van Dongen, Fiesz, Valadon, Nicolas de Staël – and works by Pierre Soulages, the Fabre museum has one of the richest painting collections in France. In addition to painting, sculpture (from Houdon to Germaine Richier) is also given ample exhibition space, as are the graphic arts – there is an exceptional collection of drawings (including Raphael, Boucher and Fragonard) – the decorative arts and temporary exhibitions.
Address: 13 rue Montpelliéret,
Tel. +33 (0)4 67 14 83 00 ∎

– are lined with some admirable mansions. The *esplanade Charles-de-Gaulle*, along the *jardin du Champ-de-Mars* and the promenade du Peyrou were both designed in the 18th century and are ideal for a stroll. The Tour de la Babote – a vestige of the town's fortifications – and the 14th-century fortified cathedral of Saint-Pierre – its façade framed by two towers – are among the oldest

monuments in the city. When you learn that Montpellier has some exceptional museums – including Musée Fabre, Musée languedocien, Musée du Vieux-Montpellier and Musée Atger – you will realise that a visit to the city requires at least two or three days.

Above
Spacious, animated and completely pedestrianised, place de la Comédie, located between the old town and the new quarter, Antigone, is the living heart of Montpellier.

NAVACELLES

This site is not only incredible, it is unique in Europe. The waters of the Vis hollowed out a crater 300m deep. Cutting through one of its own back-waters, the river also strangely isolated a rocky promontory in the centre of the cirque, on which the little village of Navacelles is nestled. The most spectacular view of this wonder of nature is from the belvedere of *La Baurne-Auriol* on the D 130 road.

Below
The cirque of Navacelles, a geological caprice of strange magnificence.

OLARGUES

Clinging to a rocky outcrop against the backdrop of Mont Caroux, Olargues seems such an unassuming little backwater – despite the beauty of its architecture and surrounding landscape – that it is amazing to discover just how rich its past has been. A Gallo-Roman town, an outpost of the Roman empire against the Celtic Arverni tribe taken by the Visigoths – it was their capital for a brief period – and then by the Saracens, with its fortified castle and ramparts, it occupies a strategic position in the Jaur valley. In fact, it was of such strategic importance that during the Albigensian Crusade Simon de Mont-fort was obliged to lay siege to it in 1210. Four centuries later, it again came to symbolise the intractability of the people of Languedoc when, in 1629, Cardinal Richelieu ordered its fortifications removed. Olargues to-day is but a peaceful village and yet its Mediaeval streets, dominated by an ancient keep, the pont du Diable (dating from 1202) and the remains of its ramparts make it well worth a stopover.

Above
A winter sunset reflected in the stones of Olargues.

FROM PALAVAS-LES-FLOTS TO MAGUELONE

Much fun has been made of the popular seaside resort of Palavas-les-Flots and its crowds of holiday-makers were cruelly caricatured by Albert Dubout. At the time of the Second World War, the resort had already become the favourite of Montpellier residents of modest means and quickly came to symbolise what the middle classes of the time scornfully called "the riff-raff on holidays". This small little fishing village deserved neither such honour nor such indignity. In spite of the ugly modern buildings nearby, it has retained its charm and the beach and quays are lively and cheerful.

About 2 1/2 miles away, near Palavas, is the cathedral of Saint-Pierre de Maguelone, built on a peninsula attached to the coastline. Heavily fortified – high façade, thick walls with few windows, battlements and arrow slits – this is all that remains of what was, in the Middle Ages, a large episcopal town and port, beachhead of the Christian world against the Saracens and refuge to several popes during the fight between Church and Empire. But competition from Montpellier, which took the bishop's seat in the 16th century, and the ravages of the Wars of Religion signalled its decline. The dismantling of its fortifications, ordered in 1622 by Cardinal Richelieu, and the subsequent dispersal of its ruins during the construction of the canal from the Rhône to Sète – the stones were sold or thrown into the bottom of the lakes – completed its transformation into a ghost town. Little remains of this glorious town swallowed up by the sand, except the solitary and nostalgic silhouette of the old cathedral, standing between sea and sky like a sentry from the past.

Above
The canal from the Rhone to Sète, near the cathedral of Maguelone, the roof of which is visible behind a clump of trees. A gate to the old abbey still stands between the canal and a lake.

Below
A fisherman on Lake Arnel spreads his nets out to dry…

NATURAL REGIONAL PARK OF HAUT-LANGUEDOC

Located on the slopes of the southernmost foothills of the Massif central, the natural regional park of Haut-Languedoc looks out over the Laugarais ridge, or *seuil*, and its plains. Extending over 260,000 hectares, it straddles the divide between the Atlantic and the Mediterranean, symbolised by the peaks of Mont Espinouse and Mont du Somail. It also straddles two regions, the Midi-Pyrénées and the Languedoc-Roussillon, and two *départements*, Tarn and Hérault. Although this book covers only the latter, the park does in fact form a cohesive ensemble that must be dealt with as a whole. It is influenced by both the Atlantic and the Mediterranean and, although located exclusively at medium altitude, it boasts exceptional biological and landscape diversity. Its granite mountain ranges, limestone cliffs, forests, pastureland, groves, scrubland, moors, fertile valleys, lakes and canyons provide shelter to a wide variety of fauna and flora. Over 2,500 living species, excluding invertebrates and lower plants, have been recorded. These include 247 species of birds, including the golden eagle, the harrier eagle and the black kite, and some rare or threatened mammals, such as the wild sheep *mouflon*, the otter and the common genet. The park's architectural heritage is also remarkable: dolmens, standing stones, abbeys, castles, churches and *oppidi*, not to mention the outstanding vernacular architecture: hilltop villages, farmhouses with slated, tiled or schist roofs, chapels, wells and wash-

Lac du Saut de Vésoles

This is a very different lakeside environment to that of Lac de la Raviège. Wild nature, moors and forests, river banks with dense vegetation and carpeted with heather – Lac du Saut de Vésoles is completely cut off from civilisation. Formed by a dam and supplied by the Bureau river, it extends over 50 hectares and it offers extraor-dinary panoramic views over the Jaur valley. There are footpaths dotted with picnic areas all around the lake. However, some areas are very steep – particularly the cliffs at the belvedere of Saut de Vésoles. Water sports are authorised but motor boats are prohibited. ■

houses greet the visitor at every turn. Hill walkers will find a wealth of sites to discover. The GR 7, GR 36, GR 71, GR 77 and GR 653 walking routes and many cycling and horse-riding ways offer unforgettable tours of some of the most beautiful natural and built landscape. Below is but a brief overview of three of the many treasures this park has to offer.

Below

With its moors, thick woods and deep valleys, the peaks of Espinouse offer wonderfully preserved landscapes.

Left page

The village of Roquebrun, on the banks of the Orb. Its exceptionally mild microclimate has earned it the nickname "little Nice".

Gorges d'Héric

Situated in the Caroux *massif*, these gorges offer some of the best walks in the park. The path winds its way past steep rock faces – Aiguilles du Rieutord, Arêtes du Coulaygue, Paroi de l'Épaule du Rieutord, Cirque de Farrière – following the tiny Héric river through a deep canyon, before veering back up towards the village of Héric, a dead-end so out of the way it has only mountain paths leading away from it. You may well encounter some wild sheep along the way. ■

Wild sheep [*mouflon*]

This ancestor of the domestic sheep became extinct in continental Europe during the 19th century. However, in 1956, a handful of specimens from Corsica were reintroduced in the Espinouse *massif*, where the combination of numerous cliffs and low snowfall provided a favourable environment. There are now over a thousand wild sheep in the area. A protected species, they were given their own 1,700-hectare national reserve in 1973. Although very timid and boasting ex-cellent eyesight, they often venture out in the daylight to feed. Adults can weigh between 25 and 40 kg and measure 70 to 75 cm to the shoulder. They have a reddish brown coat with a grey saddle patch. The male is recognisable from its imposing curved, ringed horns, the female from its white "mask". Combats between males are common during the rutting season, from mid-October to December. The ewe gives birth to one lamb – rarely two – in late April or early May. ■

PÉZENAS

A renowned wool town during the Gallo-Roman period that was later destroyed by the Great Invasions, Pézenas regained prosperity when it was bought by Saint Louis in 1261 and thus became a royal town. The right to trade granted by the king allowed the town to impose itself as a regional capital of wool. From the mid 15th century onwards, it became the home of the States General of Languedoc, which attracted aristocrats and the upper middle classes who built large homes. This golden age came to an end in 1632 when Henry de Montmorency, governor of the province, was beheaded after rebelling against Cardinal Richelieu.

A waymarked circuit (a map of which can be obtained from the Tourist Information Centre) allows visitors to discover the wonders of the "Versailles of the Languedoc", including the churches of Saint-Jean and Sainte-Ursule, Gély's barbershop – frequented by the playwright Molière when he stayed in Pézenas – the *maison des Commandeurs* and the *maison de Jacques Coeur*, and many mansions, including Sébasan, Lacoste, Alfonse, Quintin and Montmorency.

Below
The fête du Poulain, or Foal Festival, in Pézenas.

Above
The splendour of Pézenas' urban palaces – including the hôtel de Lacoste, above – reminds visitors that it was once a very rich manufacturing and administrative capital.

The abbey of Valmagne

Just over 9 miles from Pézenas, this superb ensemble comprising a church, cloister and monastic buildings was built from the 12th century onwards. Having become one of the richest and most influential abbeys in Languedoc, Valmagne was sold off as a national heritage property at the time of the Revolution, but was saved from destruction by being converted into a winemaking enterprise, a fact attested to by the barrels stored in the church. ■

Right and above
The abbey of Valmagne, an architectural treasure which only barely escaped destruction during the Revolution.

SAINT-BAUZILLE-DE-PUTOIS AND THE CAVE OF LES DEMOISELLES

Near the delightful village of Saint-Bauzille-de-Putois lies one of the most spectacular underground worlds in France. The dimensions are huge and the splendour of its decoration no less so. Everywhere, stalactites and stalagmites take on fantastic shapes and have been given evocative names such as Virgin with Child, Royal Cloak, Shoals of Jellyfish, Wall with a Thousand Columns and Organ Case. The largest chamber, appropriately called the Cathedral of the Abyss, is 52 metres high, 80 metres wide and 120 metres long and is breathtakingly majestic. However, the feelings inspired by the cave of Les Demoiselles owe as much to its beauty as to its colourful history. The Camisards sought refuge here in the early 17th century, followed later by non-juring priests during the Reign of Terror. The ease with which the cave can now be visited should not overshadow the achievements of two pioneering pot-holers Alfred Martel and Norbert Casteret, who were the first to brave the perils of this underground domain.

Below
Virgin with Child in the cave
of Les Demoiselles.

SAINT-GUILHEM-LE-DÉSERT

First of all there is the improbable beauty of the site: arid mountains, gorges, the white limestone cliffs and the green maquis and scrubland. Next there is the miraculous charm of the village, stretched into a gentle curve in the hollow of the valley, with its Romanesque tiled-roof houses and the ruins of its fortifications. The most arresting feature is the abbey, a moving masterpiece of Romanesque art, with its fortified bell tower, sculpted doorway, perfectly proportioned chevet, nave, which is so high and narrow it seems to soar heavenwards, apse, topped with a vault of breathtaking dimensions. Part of the ransacked cloister was sold and then reconstructed in New York. The abbey of Saint-Guilhem is surely one of the most moving testaments to the genius of mediaeval architects.

Top, right
Graceful and restrained, the abbey
of Saint-Guilhem is one of the
masterpieces of Romanesque art.

Right
The "Couloir Blanc", or white corridor, in
the cave of la Clamouse.

Above
Hérault is a renowned location
for canoeists.

Around Saint-Guilhem-le-Désert

The area surrounding Saint-Guilhem-le-Désert is rich in exceptional sites. You can discover the 11th-century *pont du Diable* (Devil's bridge), walk around the forest of Saint-Guilhem, using a path once used by pilgrims on their way to Santiago de Compostela, follow other paths leading to the spectacular *Cirque de l'Infernet* or the *Château du Géant* (Giant's castle), which overlooks the village and, finally, 2 1/2 miles away, visit the cave of *La Clamouse*, which, along with the cave of *Les Demoiselles*, near Ganges, is one of the finest in Languedoc. ■

SAINT-PONS-DE-THOMIÈRES

The town of Saint-Pons-de-Thomières stands at the foot of Mont du Somail and Mont de l'Espinouse, in a landscape of hills and rivers. The town dates back to the 2nd millennium B.C. but the area had already been long occupied by hunter-gatherer tribes. These tribes left behind numerous standing stones and rock paintings of such artistry that prehistorians have no hesitation in referring to the Saintponian civilisation.

Saint-Pons-de-Thomières was originally two different villages, both fortified. The oldest, Thomières – *ville Moindre* – was built on the right bank of the Jaur river. The town on the left bank, Saint-Pons – *ville Mage* – dating from the 10th century, grew up around an abbey founded by the counts of Toulouse. It was only in the 16th century that the two villages were joined together to form a single town. Many remains recall the Mediaeval past of the twin villages: the pont Notre-Dame linking the two over the Jaur, alleyways lined with 14th- and 15th-century houses, the remains of fortifications and the abbey of Saint-Pons, a former cathedral built during the 11th and 12th centuries and remodelled between the 16th and 18th centuries. With its two crenellated towers, its machicolated parapet walk and nave complete with arrow slits, it was as much a place of worship as a military endeavour – from which it got its

Left
The old fortified cathedral, both a place of worship and a military enterprise…

name of *castellum*. It boasts very rich furniture – a multicoloured marble chancel, stalls made of sculpted walnut and an organ dating from 1772, the second-earliest in France after Notre-Dame Cathedral in Paris.

Top of page
Some of the tall village houses resemble manor houses.

Right
A stela menhir at the *Musée de la Préhistoire*.

Standing stones
There are engraved standing stones dotted all over the Lacaune mountains whose meaning has been lost in the mists of time. With the sole exception of the 15-feet-high *Pierre Plantée*, they are generally around 5 feet high, close to the height of a man – perhaps intentionally. They were probably erected by Stone Age hunters from the Saintponian "civilisation", 3,000 or 4,000 B.C. Skilfully executed, the engravings portray men and women, sometimes holding an unidentifiable object. Are these figures deities, ancestors or great leaders? Nobody knows when these amazing stones will eventually reveal their secrets… ■

SALVETAT-SUR-AGOUT

How could you not fall in love with this place at first sight? Perched on a promontory overlooking the Agout river, with its alleys, covered passages and old slate-roofed houses curled around the church, La Salvetat fully merits its listing as one of the most beautiful villages in France. The Middle Ages left this former *sauveté* – the name for a village under the protectorate of the Church – with a rich heritage: the tour de Cazal, with its superb vaults, the Romanesque chapel of Saint-Étienne-de-Cavall, remnants of ramparts, fortified gates, the 12th-century pont Saint-Étienne and an 11th-century Black Virgin who is reputed to have miraculous powers. The town prospered thanks to the pilgrimage of Santiago de Compostela, for which it was a major staging post. More prosaically, it owes its reputation today to a celebrated mineral water.

Lac de la Raviège

This lake in the middle of a forest of beech and pine is like a barrier, holding back the waters of the Agout river. It extends over 400 hectares and is 7 1/2 miles long. With a bathing beach, water sports, fishing, hiking and cycling trails, Lac de la Raviège is a major regional tourist attraction. ∎

Below
The water sports facility at Boulduires on Lac de la Raviège.

SÈTE

What is the secret of this town? Compared to its handsome neighbours – and ancient rivals – Agde, Aigues-Mortes and Montpellier, Sète has neither the prestige of a long history, nor the splendour of exceptional monuments. In a region where the tiniest village has a several thousand-year old history, the "Venice of Languedoc", built from 1666 onwards, is a new town. There are of course the remains of a Gallo-Roman site and a mediaeval village, but no historic town as such. Sète owes its existence to the progressive silting up of Agde, Aigues-Mortes, Lattes – Montpellier's outer port – and Narbonne, to Jean-Baptiste Colbert's desire to give France a powerful Mediterranean port and to Pierre-Paul Riquet's desire to provide the *canal du Midi* with an outlet. Perhaps the secret is that the most recent town in Languedoc has all the colour, freshness and cheerfulness of youth. There are no moving churches or sublime mansions here. Sète's attraction lies elsewhere: in the scent of iodine and scrub, in its light, in the

Above
Le Lido seen from Pierres Blanches.

Left
La Pointe Courte and, opposite,
la Pointe Longue.

Above
The festival of Saint-Louis.

Below
During summer weekends, jousting tournaments are held on the Royal Canal in Sète.

permanent party atmosphere on its quays, in the improbable beauty of the panoramic views from the heights of *Mont Saint-Clair* and in the poignant charm of its marine cemeteries.

Sète is divided into two distinct parts. The lower town is centred around the quays, canals and bridges that make it a real lakeside town. Saint-Louis jetty, which shelters the marina, and the quays of *La Consigne* and *Le Général-Durand*, where fishing boats anchor, are the liveliest and most picturesque. Opposite, *quai Aspirant-Herber* offers a lovely view of the town. Between the town and Lake Thau, at the mouth of the canal de Sète, is a fishing village, La Pointe-Courte, that has, surprisingly, retained its character and authenticity.

The upper town has tiers of residential housing up on Mont Saint-Clair and still a lot of green areas free from construction. The marine cemetery where Paul Valéry is buried is located on the side of the mountain, facing the sea. Popular songwriter and poet Georges Brassens is buried in Le Py cemetery. At the top of the mountain, there are two sumptuous panoramas: the view from the chapel of Notre-Dame-de-la-Salette, over the lower town, the harbours and the sea, and that from Pierres-Blanches, over Lake Thau, the coastline and the Hérault mountains.

Right

A trawler returning to harbour in the
Vieux Port. Sète is the largest French
fishing port on the Mediterranean.

Below

The Royal Canal and quays of la Marine:
a multicoloured cheerfulness that makes
Sète one of the most attractive ports
on the Mediterranean.

THE VIA DOMITIA

This Roman road is the oldest in Gaul and the longest – over 300 miles long – outside the Italian peninsula. It owes its name to the proconsul Cneius Domitius Ahenobarbus who, after subjugating the region, mapped out the road and ordered its construction circa 120 B.C. It linked the Alps to the Pyrenees through Provence and Languedoc-Roussillon and remained a major thoroughfare right up to the end of the Middle Ages. The route followed by the Via Domitia was so good that many parts of it were adopted when the modern roadways were built – in particular the A9 motorway. The services available along this road rivalled anything available on motorways today. The criteria imposed on the engineers responsible for building the road included avoiding troublesome areas, ensuring that the road was as straight as possible and allowing for staging posts to provide food and lodging to users of the road every 20 miles or so. This is how Gallic towns located along the route became staging posts, as was the case with the *oppidum* of Ambrussum (see p. 56).

(see p. 56)

Above
At Saint-Thibéry, along the Via Domitia, a bridge over the Hérault river dating from Roman times.

Below
Milestones, nicknamed "Caesar's columns", near Beaucaire.

The Roman road

This was built in three layers: a deep layer of large blocks of stone to give it a stable foundation and provide drainage, a middle layer of gravel and sand, and a surface layer made of mortar, a mix of sand, fine gravel and lime. It was unpaved, except at fords and through the towns. It was 20 to 40 feet wide, with side paths along the verges for travellers on foot, horse-riders and flocks. There were mile-stones along the roadway bearing the name either of the builder or the emperor from the period the milestone was erected. Rivers were crossed by means of wooden or stone bridges and paved fords. The fact that some of these roads are still intact after over 2,000 years says something about the skill of Roman engineers. ■

Right
Part of the Via Domitia,
about half a mile from Ambrussum.

ACROSS AUDE
AND HÉRAULT:
THE CANAL DU MIDI

Between Toulouse and Lake Thau, the *Canal du Midi* is, with justification, the most famous man-made waterway in France. 150 miles long, with 350 bridges, locks, aqueducts and tunnels, Pierre-Paul Riquet's masterpiece is as much a symbol of the engineering genius of France's *grand siècle* as Versailles and is, without contest, the largest European monument ever to be listed as a World Heritage Site. Completing this gigantic canal took fifteen years, from 1666 to 1681 and 12,000 labourers working simultaneously. Pierre-Paul Riquet also had to overcome what were then considered insurmountable obstacles, inventing extraordinarily audacious technical solutions, such as canal aqueducts, water steps and canal tunnels. Coming from Toulouse, the canal enters Languedoc at the *Seuil de Naurouze* – its culminating point, where water from the *Montagne Noire* is collected. From here, 120 miles of canal meander through Aude and Hérault – with a height difference of 189m

Above, left
In the shade of plane trees, near Paraza.

Above, right
The "staircase" of Fonsérannes, in Béziers.

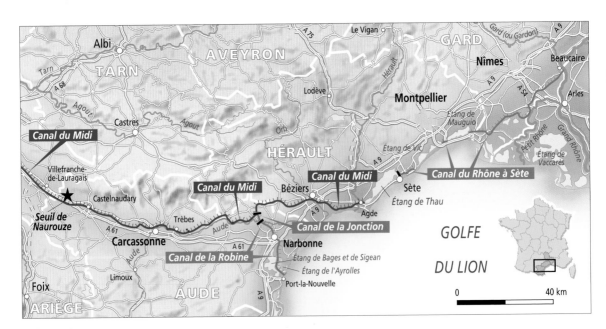

compensated for by forty-eight locks – to the Mediterranean. If you follow its course, you will come across some of the most beautiful towns in Languedoc, villages with undiscovered charm, and can admire the ingenious works designed by Riquet.

Apart from the above-mentioned towns of Castelnaudary, Carcassonne, Béziers and Agde, you should not miss the villages of Trèbes, Homps, Argens-Minervois, Paraza, Somail, Argeliers and Capestang – all of which have a treasure to offer, whether fortified castle, Templar outpost, Gothic church, Romanesque chapel, mediaeval ramparts or episcopal palace.

The most outstanding works of Riquet – or Vauban, who succeeded him – are, undeniably, the canal aqueduct at Trèbes across the Orbiel river; the over-flow basin and aqueduct at Argent Double, near La Redorte; the canal aqueduct of la Repudre – the oldest in the world – not far from Paraza; the canal aqueduct at Cesse, near Port-la-Robine; the tunnel at Malpas, at the foot of Ensérune; the colossal water staircase at Fonsérannes – where 8 successive locks compensate for a height difference of 25m under the walls of Béziers – and finally the famous round lock at Agde.

Below
The port of Somail, a former stopover point for horse-drawn barges.

Above
The mouth of the canal at Lake Thau.

Lozère

Situated between Margeride, Aubrac,
Grands Causse and Cévennes, this is the old country of Gévaudan,
severe and superb like its legends.

Left page

The waterfall of Déroc, one of the most popular natural sites in Aubrac.

Lozère has vast spaces which are practically uninhabited. It is a seemingly limitless plain, with pared-back mountains battered by the wind, forests where wolves still roam, gorges where vultures fly overhead, under which the waters of the Lot, the Allier and the Tarn rivers foam, and villages made of granite. This raw splendour, where nature is respected and where man has left – and will continue to leave, let us hope – only the slightest traces.

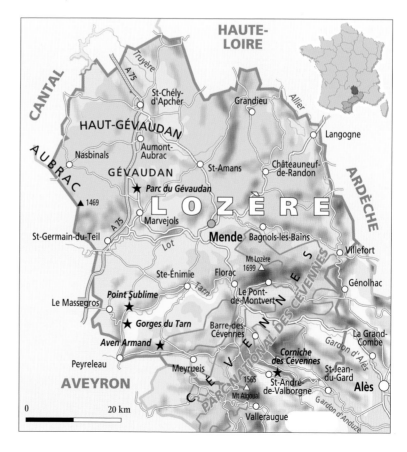

AUBRAC

What can be said about the bald landscapes of Aubrac, about its endless
expanses of turf, moors and pastureland criss-crossed with streams, except that they are unique in France?
This is another world, a world of
steppes, where you would not be sur-
prised to see yurts and nomads on
horseback, where it is easy to believe
that the legendary Beast of Gévaudan
still roams. The only indication that
man ever adapted to this untameable
environment is the occasional *buron*,
a dry-stone shepherds' hut.

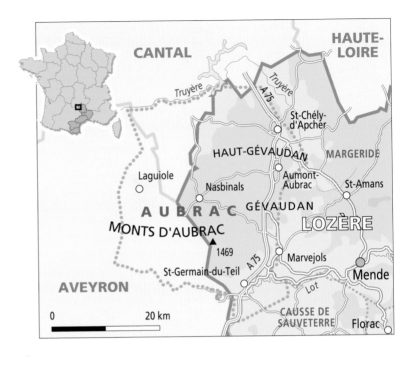

Below
Aubrac cows and calves in pasture.

There are villages in the middle of nowhere, admirable in their simplicity, with stone houses and schist roofs and little Romanesque churches: Marchastel, Fau-de-Peyre, Chirac, Prinséjuols or Aubrac, which is home to the remains of an abbey of hospitaller monks who welcomed and escorted pilgrims on their way to Santiago de Compostela. The larger village of Nasbinals – with 500 inhabitants, this ranks as almost a town in these parts – is home to a Romanesque church built in the 11th and 12th centuries, which has a very handsome octagonal bell tower.

In the heart of Gévaudan country, Marvejols is the capital of the region, with almost 6,000 inhabitants. Apart from its ancient streets lined with beautiful houses – and, incidentally, the omnipresent memories of the Beast of Gévaudan – the town has also retained some very handsome fortified gates – Chanelles, Théron and Soubeyran – each of which are defended by two round towers and battlements. There is also a 17th-century church, Notre-Dame-de-la-Carce, with a statue of the Virgin, which is the object of particular veneration. Around 7 miles from Marvejols is the *château de la Baume*, a classical-style castle of dark granite

Above
A steppe-like landscape with immense horizons…

Below
The lake of Saint-Andéol, with a perimeter of over a mile, is the largest in Aubrac.

which is considered the most handsome in Lozère, to the extent that it has been nicknamed the "Versailles of Gévaudan". Not far from the town – about 6 miles away – the animal park "Les Loups du Gévaudan" is well worth a visit, not only because you can see up to a hundred wolves living in semi-liberty, but also because here you will find out that the famous Beast was almost certainly not a giant wolf but more likely a human serial killer.

Below
The château de la Baume,
the "Versailles of the Gévaudan".

Above
The wolf, the symbolic
animal of the Gévaudan.

Right page
The *transhumance* festival, at the col
de Bonnecombe: an enduring tradition…

THE *CAUSSES*

Arid, subjected to a rigorous climate and particularly harsh winters, these high *causses*, cut through with deep canyons, contain more sheep than people. Two of the four *Grands Causses* – the Méjean and the Sauveterre, separated by the gorges du Tarn – belong to Lozère. The others, Larzac and the *Causse Noir* are mostly in Aveyron.

Left page

The Sabot de Malepeyre, sculpted by water and wind on the causse de Sauveterre.

Below

The causse, or limestone plateau, of Méjean: a bitter, hostile land, which counts more sheep than humans…

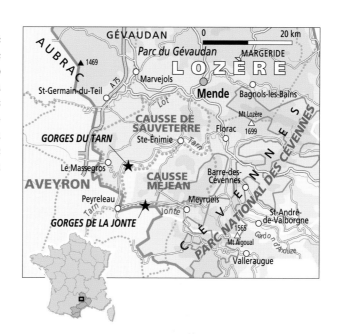

The *Causse de Sauveterre* is the least desolate, with wooded areas and tilled fields, especially in the south-western part. In the village of Sauveterre, after which the *causse* is named, many dry-stone houses with schist roofs, typical of the local architecture, have been preserved. La Canourgue, criss-crossed with little channels, with its alleyways and arcades, is a peaceful and charming place to stop. Its church, Saint-Martin – the remains of a monastery founded in the 7th century and which gave birth to the town – is a cheerful mix of Romanesque, Gothic and Renaissance architecture.

At an average altitude of 1,000m, the *causse* of Méjean is a veritable human desert. There are 0.5 inhabitants per square mile, in other words, its density is equivalent to that in the Sahel regions of sub-Saharan Africa. There are a few hamlets and huge farms: the one in Hyelzas, near the sinkhole of Armand has been converted into an eco-museum. However, farming is rare and restricted to the small *dolina*, and there are endless steppes which stretch towards the horizon. Visitors must see the two

natural curiosities of the *causse*, namely Nîmes-le-Vieux, which is not a town but an extraordinary mass of rocks that looks like a ruined town from a distance, and the sinkhole of Armand, at the bottom of which, after passing through an 188m-long tunnel by funicular railway, visitors will find a colossal cave 75m below ground – comparable in size to the cathedral of Notre-Dame-de-Paris – decorated with a profusion of limestone formations and called the "Virgin Forest".

Left
The hall of the "Virgin Forest" in the sinkhole of Armand.

Above, left
A roadside cross on the causse de Sauveterre.

Above, right
The cross of Buffre, on the causse of Méjean.

Right page
Seen from a distance, the rocky mass of Nîmes-le-Vieux looks like the ruins of a huge city.

THE CÉVENNES COAST ROAD

Winding over a peak between the two Gardon rivers – the Gardon de Sainte-Croix and the Gardon de Saint-Jean – the Cévennes coast road, which links Florac to Saint-Jean-du-Gard, allows travellers to discover one of the most spectacular landscapes of the region. Most of this 33-mile-long road, which can easily be covered in less than two hours, is in Lozère, the entrance to Gard being a few miles from Saint-Jean. The road follows an ancient track, which was doubtless already there during the time of the Gauls and originally used by shepherds moving to summer pastures. It became a royal road in the 18th century to allow troops through to repress the revolt of the Camis-

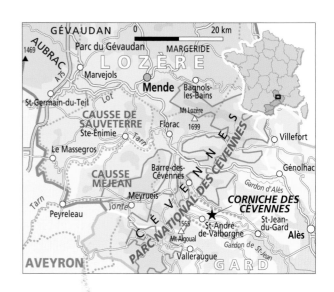

Below

The Corniche des Cévennes, near Pompidou.

ards, insurgent 17th-century French Protestants.

The starting point of the excursion is Florac, a peaceful town situated at the foot of the Méjean *causse*. Around the small Vibron river, which passes through the town, there are narrow alleyways and ancient houses with high façades, which are well preserved and full of charm. Its 17th-century castle, flanked by two round towers, today houses the offices of Cévennes National Park. To the south of Florac, the road follows the Tarnon river upstream along the foot of Méjean and then crosses Saint-Laurent-de-Trèves. From this village overlooking the valley, the view of Mont Aigoual, Mont Lozère and the Causse Noir, Sauveterre and Méjean is unforgettable. Nearby is a listed site containing dinosaur footprints. After the col de Rey, the road goes into the *can* of Hospitalet, a wild plateau of moors, scree and sinkholes, the last stronghold of the Camisard resistance, which offers several vantage points over the Française valley, one of the most beautiful in the Cévennes. You could make a short detour (under 2 miles) to visit the village of Barre-des-Cévennes, with its traditional houses and church of Notre-Dame-de-l'Assomption. Returning to the peak, you pass through the picturesque villages of Pompidou and Saint-Roman-de-Tousque. The road next goes along the top of the Borgne valley before reaching the col de l'Exil – from where the banished Camisards are reputed to have taken one last look at their country – and then the col de Saint-Pierre, which is the start of the magnificent winding descent to Saint-Jean-du-Gard.

Above
A Cévennes farm and its *bancels* or *faisses* (terraced fields).

Right
Montjoie (standing stone used as a landmark for travellers) on the *Can de l'Hospitalet* plateau.

THE *GORGES DU TARN* AND *GORGES DE LA JONTE*

There are few places in Europe to match the splendour of these landscapes carved out of the *causses*. There are breathtakingly high canyons, defiles hemmed in by rocky walls nearly 600m high, villages clinging to the side of escarpments or huddled against cliffs and the ruins of fortified castles perched above the abyss.

The grandest part of the *gorges du Tarn* is situated in the thirty or so miles between Ispagnac and Le Rozier. Ispagnac, the "garden of Lozère", houses one of the most beautiful Romanesque churches in the region, as well as Gothic houses and the remains of a castle. Downstream is the 14th-century bridge of Quézac, the 16th-century castles of Rocheblave and Charbonnières, the village of Castelbouc, with its castle ruins perched on a rocky ledge, and the fortress of Prades, also built on an escarpment. In a narrow passage of the canyon, Sainte-Enimie, with its 12th-century church, ancient monastic ruins and cobblestone alleyways, has retained all its mediaeval character. Next there is Saint-Chély-du-Tarn, nestled at the foot of the cliffs; Pougnadoires, with tiers of houses on the side of a cirque; La Malène, an ancient crossroads of *transhumance*, the traditional migration of shepherds moving their flocks to summer pastures – overlooked by the rocky mass of *La Barre, Les Détroits* – a veritable corridor between two 400 m-high cliffs – and the cirque of

Above
Absent since the beginning of the 20th century, the wild vulture has been successfully reintroduced.

Below, left
Meyrueis, gateway to the gorges de la Jonte.

Below, right
Sainte-Énimie, "capital" of the gorges du Tarn.

Left
The village of Castelbouc.

Below
The entry to the gorges du Tarn,
in le Rozier.

Baumes, with its masses of rocks and needles. Between Vignes and Le Rozier, finally, the gorges widen but the high cliffs, cirques and promontories crowned with ruins are just as spectacular as before. All along the route, well-placed belvederes offer extraordinary vantage points. The *Point Sublime*, above the cirque of Baumes, is, rightly, the most famous.

The *gorges de la Jonte* are shorter – about 12 miles – and less imposing, but they are just as spectacular. Leaving Meyrueis, an attractive town with remains of fortifications, ancient alleyways and houses, head towards the hamlet of Douzes, dominated by the *roc Saint-Gervais*, topped by a Romanesque chapel, then towards Le Truel, a beautiful, tiny village. A little downstream from here is the *belvedere des Terrasses*, which, apart from offering sumptuous panoramic views, can be used as a vantage point for vultures, reintroduced around thirty years ago.

MENDE

Located at the borders of Auvergne and Languedoc, the administrative capital of Lozère is a small, seldom-mentioned town. This is unjust, as it has a lot of beautiful architecture and really peaceful charm to offer. Its prosperity during the early Middle Ages was due to its privileged position at the crossroads of the great trading routes linking Languedoc to the Auvergne and to the fact that it had imposed itself as the capital of Gévaudan. It was made a bishopric in the 9th century and, in the 12th century, the king of France granted temporal power over the town to the bishops, which they retained up until the Revolution. The cathedral was only built in 1369, thanks to the support of Pope Urban V, who was born locally. It was completely destroyed by the Protestants during the Wars of Religion and was faithfully rebuilt during the following century. The old quarters, with cobblestone alley-

Below
Horses in semi-liberty
in Margeride.

Below
The cathedral of Notre-Dame-et-Saint-Privat in Mende.

Left
The bridge of Notre-Dame in Mende.

Bottom
The legend of the beast gave
rise to a wealth of popular imagery.

ways, the Penitents' chapel and its *Musée d'Art sacré, tour d'Auriac* – the last remains of the fortifications – the 13th-century synagogue, the 12th century bridge of Notre-Dame, built over the Lot river – all of these things justify Mende's classification as a "ville d'art" (Town of Art). Overlooking it all is the cathedral of Notre-Dame-et-Saint-Privat, with its two asymmetric spires. Inside the cathedral there are some pieces of note, including a Black Virgin which may have been brought back from the Holy Land by the crusaders.

The Beast of Gévaudan

Between 1764 and 1767, a monster terrorised the entire Gévaudan area. Its often horribly mangled victims – there were 250 attacks, causing 101 fatalities and wounding 70 – were mostly women and children. Was the Beast a rabid wolf, lynx or wildcat from some far-flung region? Some spoke of a demon or werewolf, while the clergy intimated divine punishment. Wildlife wardens and huntsmen searched in vain. In 1765, the Harquebus Bearer to King Louis XV, Antoine de Beauterne, sent to the region with forty men, killed a gigantic wolf. For a few weeks,

Gévaudan thought it was saved, until the carnage recommenced. In June 1767, another large wolf was killed with consecrated bullets by a huntsman, Jean Chastel. Was it the Beast? Probably, because the attacks suddenly ceased. But the mystery remains: the remains of killed wolves, sent to Paris for examination, arrived in such a state of decomposition that it was impossible to identify them with certainty. And the rumour persisted that the Beast was actually a man, a diabolical psychopath so cunning that the murders were attributed to wild animals. ■

Margeride

Mende is the gateway to Margeride, a granite mountain range with grandiose landscapes: desolate plateaux, deep forests, sparse villages scattered over vast depopulated expanses. This land was favoured by the European bison, which prospered here in semi-liberty in a natural park at Sainte-Eulalie-en-Margeride. Some sites are worth a visit, such as the *gorges de la Truyère*, accessible only on foot or by mountain bike, or the very pretty village of Châteauneuf-de-Randon, where Bertrand du Guesclin, the Breton warrior, died. ■

MARVEJOLS

An old rival to Mende – it was, briefly, the capital of Gévaudan before ceding the title to Mende – Marvejols, an old fiefdom of the counts of Toulouse, finally came under royal authority only in the 12th century. Contrary to its neighbour, which was ruled by the bishops, it was always administered directly by the kings of France. The town sided with the Huguenots during the Wars of Religion and was sacked by the Catholic troops of the Duke de Joyeuse: three quarters of the population were massacred, the town set ablaze and the fortifications destroyed. However, Henry IV of Navarre had the town rebuilt in 1601, turning it into a Protestant stronghold. When the Edict of Nantes was revoked, and again during the Camisard war, many of Marvejols' inhabitants fled to safety. Those that stayed behind were forced to recant, while others were imprisoned or executed. Marvejols has managed to retain a rich heritage from these troubled times. The 17th-century church of Notre-Dame-de-la-Carce, the streets and squares lined with old houses in the pedestrianised heart of the town, its three fortified gates flanked with machicolated towers and schist roofs – porte de Soubeyran, porte du Théron and porte de Chanelles – make it a beautiful town of art and history.

Top of page
The statue of Notre-Dame-de-la-Carce in the church of the same name.

Left
The porte de Chanelle in Marvejols.

MONT AIGOUAL AND *MONT LOZÈRE*

Standing firm against the wind and the fog, these mountains watch over Lozère like a couple of sentries.

With an altitude of 1,567m, *Mont Aigoual* is the highest point in the Cévennes. Whichever route you take to reach it – via Espérou, Le Vigan, Meyrueis or Valleraugue – the countryside is superb. There are many walks on its slopes, two of which are the *Sentier des Botanistes* – a 1/2 mile circuit around the summit, which crosses the "Hort de Dieu" arboretum – and the path of the "4,000 steps". From the summit the view extends from the Mediterranean to the Alps.

Mont Lozère – nicknamed the Bald Mountain because of its bare summit – is 1,699m high. Take the GR 7 – an old sheep track for bringing flocks to la Margeride – to see the most characteristic countryside and villages.

Don't miss the hamlets on the slopes of the mountain and in its foothills – La Fage for example – whose "storm bells" used to guide lost travellers, the pretty villages of Saint-Julien-de-Tournel and Pont-de-Montvert – which is home to the *Maison du Mont Lozère* – and the strange universe of "Cham des Bondons", a barren plateau dominated by the rocky hillock of the *puech*, which has hundreds of menhirs.

Below, left
Weather station at the summit of Mont Aigoual.

Above
On the slopes of Mont Lozère...

Below, right
A standing stone on the Cham des Bondons.

Cévennes National Park

Opened in 1970, the park extends to the heart of the Cévennes and covers an area of 91,500ha (80% in Lozère, 20% in Gard), surrounded by a peripheral area of 235,000ha. It is the only populated French National Park, with about 600 people living in 52 towns. It encompasses mainly Mont Aigoual, Mont Lozère and Mont Lingas, the Française, Longue and Borgne valleys, the *causse* of Méjean and the Bougès range. In 1985, Unesco declared the park a World Biosphere Reserve. And with good reason: since the 19th century, the park has been spared from the excesses of intensive farming. At the same time, the reduction in areas devoted to tillage and the increasing encroachment of moors and forests have made it one of the richest areas in terms of biological diversity in Europe today. The outstanding variety of landscape and environments – forests, moors, plateaus, rivers and torrents, granite, limestone and schist soil – is complemented by a variety of wildlife that is no less exceptional: stags, beavers, wild sheep, otters, eagles, vultures, capercaillies – almost half of the vertebrate species in France can be seen in the park. Rural depopulation has also played its part in the preservation of the rural habitat. Cévennes houses are always in perfect harmony with the landscape: solid, bulky, nestling into the surrounding contours for protection and built using locally sourced materials – limestone from the Causses, granite from the area around Mont Lozère and schist from the Protestant Cévennes. Further information about the park is available at the *château de Florac*. ∎

Left page, top
In the heart of the park, a typical Cévennes landscape.
Left page, bottom
In this overview of Florac, the castle with its round towers is clearly visible. The castle houses the visitors' centre, *Maison du Parc*.
Below
A hay loft on Mont Lozère, restored by the National Park.

PONT-DE-MONTVERT

To see today, so peaceful, its old houses reflected in the Tarn river, it is difficult to believe that this peaceful village was at the centre of a bloody repression of the Camisard revolt. The charm of its streets and neighbouring Protestant and Catholic churches are far removed from the awkward co-existence – if you could use the word – of the two religions. The bridge, flanked by a clock tower near which the Abbé du Chayla died, after being stabbed fifty-four times, is airily elegant. Above all, the Mont Lozère ecomuseum is a must-see. This museum is a hymn to the *cévenol* soul, its ruggedness and humanity, its thirst for independence and freedom, as fierce as the landscape that wrought it.

Above
It was from this bridge that the body of the Abbé du Chayla, who was stabbed to death, was thrown into the Tarn…

VILLEFORT AND ITS LAKE

Clinging to the foothills of Mont Lozère, the small, pretty town of Villefort is well worth a look, with its 14th- and 15th-century facades emblazoned with lintels and coats of arms, its wash-house and bridge and the pont Saint-Jean. However, its main attraction is the man-made lake to which it gave its name: 137 hectares, a bathing beach, a water sports centre, magnificent wild landscape – this majestic lake is a highly popular resort.

Right
This bathing beach takes nothing away from the wild beauty of the lake.

The Camisard insurgency

Fierce and rebellious, the *pays cévenol* long resisted subjugation by both king and church. Resisting the authority of the monarchs who sought to impose their rule by force, it also long withstood the Catholic church's hold over souls and minds, adopting in turn all the heresies – Arianism, the Waldenses, the Cathars – that crossed Languedoc during the Middle Ages. Not surprisingly, the Reformation in the 16th century also took hold here. Catholic repression during the Wars of Religion was harsh, resulting in massacres in Mende, La Canourgue and Marvejols. While the Edict of Nantes restored an uneasy peace (if not tolerance), when it was revoked by Louis XIV in 1685, Cévennes was set ablaze. In Pont-de-Monvert (see below), the sinister Abbé du Chayla persecuted the populace with dragonnades, tortures, imprisonments and hangings, and sent many men to the galleys. His harshness induced such hate that he was assassinated in 1702 by a man called Esprit Séguier. The Camisard insurgency – so called because of the white shirts (*camisa* in Languedocien) worn by the insurgents – had begun. Intimately acquainted with the terrain, the Camisards mounted an insurrection against the royal armies, using guerrilla tactics such as ambush and hit-and-run raids, and routing them completely. Unable to achieve military victory, Marshal Montrevel organised what became known as the "great burning of the Cévennes": villages, hamlets, farms, barns and harvests were destroyed and burnt down, while the population was forcibly removed to a handful of fortified villages or executed en masse when there was the slightest suspicion that they were helping the rebels. Any Camisards that were captured were summarily executed. Eventually, Marshal de Villars negotiated the partial surrender of the insurgents in May 1704, in exchange for a general amnesty, freedom of worship – albeit only in private – and damages for those whose houses had been burnt down. However, many rebels refused to surrender and it was only in 1705 that relative peace was restored. Villars' promises were never kept and the region rose up sporadically throughout the first half of the 18th century, although the fighting was never as intense as during the period 1702-1705. ■

The roads
to Santiago de Compostela

The largest pilgrimage destination in the Western world for many centuries, Santiago de Compostela, in Galicia, has drawn hundreds of thousands – or even millions – of men and women from all over Europe. Curiously, while increasing secularisation meant falling numbers of pilgrims walking to the shrine of the Apostle as far back as the 18th century, the roads of Santiago de Compostela have witnessed a revival over the last few decades among a different type of pilgrim – walkers. While many are doubtless guided by faith, most are attracted by the beauty of the countryside traversed by these roads. In France, there are four major roads leading to the Pyrenees, which merge into a single roadway, the Camino francés, across the Spanish border. The Via Turonensis went from Paris, the Via Lemovicensis from Vézelay, the Via Podensis from Puy-en-Velay and the Via Tolosana from Arles. The Via Tolosana passed through Montpellier, Toulouse, Auch and Pau before reaching the col du Somport. The eastern part of the road crossed Languedoc, with major staging points at Saint-Gilles, Montpellier, Saint-Guilhem-le-Désert, Lodève, Lunas, Saint-Gervais-sur-Mare, Murat-sur-Vèbre and La Salvetat-sur-Agout and is now integrated into the GR 653 walking route.

There are, however, many variants to the Via Tolosana. Pilgrims sometimes came off the main route to pay their respects to a particular saint. The outcome is that, in addition to the GR 653, there is a veritable warren of pilgrim routes, many of them official GR walking routes, throughout Languedoc-Roussillon. What better way to discover the region than via these routes, dotted with monasteries and churches – many of which were used as dormitories – hospices, lazarettos and towns offering sanctuary to the pilgrims? For more information see www.chemins-compostelle.com or www.gr-infos.com ∎

Lozère on foot

This mountainous, barely inhabited region is ideal for walking. In the Aubrac, Margeride, Cévennes and Causses, walkers cross landscapes unchanged since the time when the only people to be found here were pilgrims on their way to Santiago de Compostela or shepherds moving to summer pastures. The GR 6 and 7 footpaths cross the region from north to south. In Aubrac, you can choose between the GR 65 – which retraces one of the routes to Santiago de Compostela – and the GR "Tour de l'Aubrac". The GR 66 brings you around the Aigoual, the GR 68 around Mont Lozère. The GR 67 brings you around the Cévennes and, if you combine paths GR 6 and GR 60, you will discover the *causses* of Méjean and Sauveterre. ■

Left page and below
The sheep tracks of Aubrac, ancient *transhumance* pathways used by shepherds moving their flocks to summer pastures, has been given new life by hillwalkers.

Above
Spurred on by faith or simply the pleasure of discovering wonderful countryside, increasing numbers of walkers walk along the old pilgrim roads to Santiago de Compostela every year.

Pyrénées-Orientales

More than a *département*, this is a land with a strong identity, which still remembers its past as part of the ancient kingdom of Catalonia and remains steeped in an original culture, very different from that of Languedoc.

Left page

Collioure and the bell tower/beacon of Notre-Dame-des-Anges.

"The Pyrenees are no more," said King Louis XIV after the treaty of 1659. If they ever did exist for the Catalans of France and Spain, they have been more of a link than a border. Between the summits of Canigou and Carlit, the uplands of Cerdagne and Capcir, the valleys of Conflent and Vallespir, the hills and slopes of Aspres and Fénouillèdes, the creeks and harbours of the Vermilion Coast, the castles, abbeys, age-old villages and *villes d'art* make up an abundantly rich heritage.

LE CANIGOU

Perhaps due to a mapmaker's calculation error, this mountain was long thought to be the highest peak in the Pyrenees. Nonetheless, Le Canigou has always been held by Catalans to be a sacred mountain, the symbol of their cultural unity in spite of the border. Thus, every year, French and Spanish Catalans meet at the summit to light a bonfire on Saint John's Eve, the summer solstice. Ascending Le Canigou (three to four hours' walk there and back) is not difficult, as long as the weather conditions are favourable. From its summit, at an altitude of 2,784m, there is a magnificent panoramic view embracing the peaks of the Pyrenees, the Corbières, the Albères and the summits of the Costa Brava.

Below
Vernet-les-Bains and Mont Canigou, the sacred mountain of the Catalans.

CASTELNOU

With its light coloured-stone which turns golden in the sun, Castelnou is surely one of the prettiest villages in Roussillon. The best way to visit is on foot, after crossing its fortified enclosure via a gate flanked by two towers. There are cobblestone alleyways with stairways here and there, narrow-faced houses and craft shops – everything here has an air of authenticity. On the mound dominating the village, the 10th-century castle emerges from behind the trees in its park, sturdy and austere. It is a unique place, as graceful as an illumination…

Thuir

Just under 4 miles from Castelnou, Thuir is the smallest capital in the stony terraces of the Aspres. Apart from the mediaeval quarter and the church of Notre-Dame, which houses an exceptional 12th-century Virgin, don't miss the Byrrh cellars, where many aperitifs are prepared, such as Cinzano, Dubonnet and of course Byrrh, made with sweet wine and cinchona. Here you will also see an oak barrel that can hold a million litres and is reputedly the largest in the world. ■

Top of page
Castelnou, which has all
the grace of an illumination…

Middle of page
The exquisite simplicity of the chapel of la Piétat, in Thuir.

Bottom of page
This oak barrel in the Byrrh cellars is the largest in the world, containing a million litres.

COLLIOURE

It is no surprise to learn that this little fishing port, famous for centuries for its anchovies, attracted so many famous painters, namely Matisse, Derain, Braque and Picasso. Its location between sea and mountain is one of the most beautiful on the Vermilion Coast. Collioure has steep, cobblestone alleyways and pink façades in the Mouré quarter, painted barges dancing on the water in the old port, nets drying on the quays, all of it bathed in an indescribably pure light. However, the town does not only offer a lively, cheerful atmosphere, it also has some exceptional monuments, including the *château royal*, built at the beginning of the 14th century by the kings of Majorca, then for-

tified in the 17th century by Marshal Vauban; the 17th-century church of Notre-Dame-des-Anges, whose round bell tower was once the town's beacon and which contains unexpected riches and furniture, in particular nine retables in the Catalan Baroque style. A fun way to discover Collioure is to follow the "chemin du Fauvisme", which is interspersed with twenty reproductions of paintings by Derain and Matisse, placed at the exact points where they were painted.

Above
The port of Collioure, dominated by the castle of the kings of Majorca, opens out onto one of the most beautiful and varied coastlines in the Mediterranean.

Below
Casks of Banyuls ageing in the open air.

Around Collioure
To the south of Collioure, Port-Vendres and Banyuls are also worth a visit, Port-Vendres for its Spanish charm and lively quaysides, Banyuls for its old quarters and colourful houses, cellars where the famous local wine matures, and for the mas *Maillol*, where one of the greatest sculptors of the last century, Aristide Maillol, worked and died. ∎

ELNE

Up to 1602, when Perpignan took over the role, this ancient town, which was first Iberian, then Roman – its name comes from Helena, the mother of the Emperor Constantine – was the episcopal seat and capital of Roussillon for over a thousand years. Completely enclosed by ramparts – from which there is a lovely view over the surrounding countryside – the town has a remarkable Romanesque building in the cathedral of Sainte-Eulalie. The cathedral's façade looks like a fortress, with rare openings and crenellated towers and it houses some beautiful pieces, such as a 14th-century retable and an 11th-century altar. The adjoining 12th- and 14th-century cloister is one of the best preserved in the region and its capitals are masterpieces of mediaeval sculpture.

EUS

According to its inhabitants, this is the prettiest village in France.

In any event, it is certainly one of the prettiest. Perched on a sunny hillside on the Conflent border, the entire village of Eus has been listed as a historical monument. This treasure lacks nothing: it has a gorgeous backdrop of mountains, ramparts, ancient houses and a Romanesque church.

The spas

There are many spas in the Pyrénées-Orientales, some of which have been in use since Gallo-Roman times. Less than 4 miles from Eus is Molitg-les-Bains, dominated by the ruins of the *château de Paracollis* and home to a beautiful Romanesque church. This is without contest one of the most charming spas in the region. ■

Below
The cathedral of Sainte-Eulalie in Elne, with a detail from one of its capitals.

Top, right
Eus, a treasure of a village in Conflent.

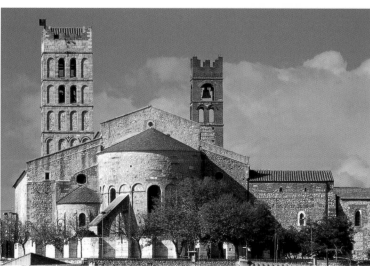

FONT-ROMEU
AND LA CERDAGNE

Many sports-lovers will have heard of Font-Romeu, where top-class athletes have found the ideal climactic conditions for preparing for competition. It must be said that La Cerdagne, a high plain surrounded by mountains where the resort is located has many assets: the average altitude is 1,200m, there are over 3,000 hours of sunshine a year, pure air and undisturbed wildlife. In brief, this is a walker's paradise. Add cultural tourism to sports tourism and you'll need to prepare for a proper stay rather than a lightning visit. One of the nicest ways to discover La Cerdagne is to climb aboard the "Yellow Train" (see page 138). Apart from astonishing landscapes – forests, masses of rocks, torrents and narrow valleys – you will discover some wonderful villages, such as Dorres, Eyne, Llo, Planès, with its clover-shaped church, and Llivia, a "forgotten" Spanish enclave in France. Visit the solar furnace at Odeillo – the most powerful in the world – and make sure not to miss Mont-Louis, a stronghold built by Vauban with ramparts that look like they were built only yesterday...

Right

The track to Roc de la Calme, in Font-Romeu.

Above
The valley of the Cerdagne.

Above
The solar furnace in Odeillo.

GALAMUS

Admirable, stupefying, incomparable... words fail to describe the *Gorges of Galamus*. Imagine a narrow defile of dizzying depths at the bottom of which a torrent foams over a mass of rocks. And, pinned to the side of the cliff, balancing on a miniscule promontory, there is a small hermitage with a chapel, which can only be reached via an underground stairway. Hermits lived here from the 6th or 7th century onwards. Maybe faith is a good cure for vertigo...

Right
The hermitage of Galamus, suspended over the abyss...

ILLE-SUR-TÊT

This is one of those towns which seduce at first sight, with its well-kept mediaeval quarter, the remains of its fortified enclosure, its Baroque church and its hospice of Saint-Jacques, which houses a *centre d'Art sacré* with astonishingly rich collections. But Ille-sur-Têt is mostly famous for its Organs, a unique geological site in the Pyrenees. Over an area of several miles stand the fantastic silhouettes of fairy-like chimneys sculpted by erosion, with the summit of Canigou in the background.

Left
The Organs of Ille-sur-Têt,
with the Canigou in the background.

Right page, top
The porte de France, in Mont-Louis.

Right page, bottom
A watchtower in the ramparts
of Mont-Louis.

MONT-LOUIS

In the 17th century Vauban, the greatest French military architect ever, remodelled or restored over three hundred strongholds along the kingdom's borders. He also built nine entirely from scratch, seven of which remain intact. They include Mont-Louis, which is one of the best-preserved examples and which has been proposed for listing as a World Heritage Site. Built 5000 feet above sea level (making it the highest fortified town in France) to guard the Spanish border after the Peace of the Pyrenees of 1659, it represents "an exceptional, monumental ensemble, as it has preserved almost all of its walls and embankments, together with its walled village with its original layout and great glacis in front of the citadel itself" (report by Monuments historiques, October 2002). The town, dominated by a many-sided citadel, is laid out according to a grid pattern of eight streets and is completely enclosed by ramparts. Apart from the fact that it clearly illustrates the architectural genius of Vauban in a confined space, Mont-Louis has a fine 18th-century church and a rare example of a tread wheel used to draw water (there are only two others extant in France).

THE NATURAL REGIONAL PARK OF PYRÉNÉES CATALANES

Inaugurated in March 2004, this is the latest area in Languedoc-Roussillon to be designated a natural park. It extends over a huge, sparsely-populated area – 137,100 hectares, or almost one third of the département of Pyrénées-Orientales with a population of just 21,000, distributed in 64 districts. Forests cover half of the park. which extends over three mountainous regions – Cerdagne, Capcir and Conflent. It is buttressed by massifs – Mont Canigou, Campcardos, Carlit and Puigmal – which rise 3,000 metres above sea level. The park is also home to five classified natural sites – Bouillouses lake and the Désert du Carlit, the cirque, or corrie, of the Camporells lakes, Lake Lanoux, the gorges de la Carança and the slopes of Mont Canigou – seven natural reserves – Conat, Eynes, Jujols, Mantet, Nohèdes, Py and Nyer – and 58% of its territory is listed in the Natura 2000 network.

Its splendid landscapes – high plateaux, deep valleys, mountains with grandiose cliffs, high-altitude lakes – its hilltop villages and out-of-the-way hamlets, the variety of its flora – almost a thousand plant species recorded – and of its fauna – izards, marmots, ptarmigans, capercaillies and bearded vultures – its preserved way of life and exceptional sunshine make it a wonderful place for walking routes for both strollers and hardened hikers, such as the GR 10 route that leads to Mont Canigou, the Carança massif, Lake Carlit and Lake Lanoux. However, the park is not only a protected natural environment. It has a strong cultural identity – the Catalan language is still spoken here – and architectural heritage – for example, the Romanesque churches of Ria, Ur, Corneilla-de-Conflent, Saint-Michel-de-Cuxa (see p. 135), Saint-Martin-du-Canigou (see p. 135) among others, the fortified towns of Mont-Louis, (see p. 129) and Villefranche-de-Conflent (see p. 139), both of which have been proposed for listing as World Heritage Sites – all of which make it a high point of any visit.

Left
The village of Py, in the heart of one of the seven natural reserves in the park.

Natura 2000

With the Natura 2000 network, Europe undertook an ambitious project to build an ecological network with the dual aim of preserving biological diversity and enhancing natural heritage.

The two most important objectives are defined in the 1979 Birds Directive and 1992 Habitats Directive, which set out the regulatory basis for the European ecological network.

The Birds Directive requires the long-term conservation of wild bird species in the European Union and targets 181 vulnerable species and sub-species requiring particular attention. Over 3,000 sites have been classified as Special Protection Areas (SPAs) by Member States. The Habitats Directive sets out a framework for Community-wide initiatives for the conservation of other species of wildlife and their habitats. This directive lists over 200 types of natural habitats, 200 animal species and 500 plant species of Community interest that require protection. Special Areas of Conservation (SACs), of which there are currently 20,000, representing 12% of territory in the EU, provide protection to these vulnerable habitats and species. ■

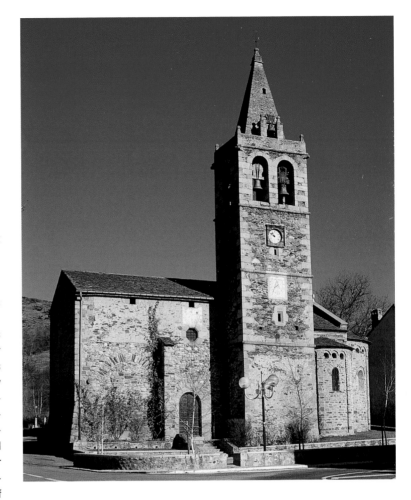

Above
The Romanesque church of Ur in the Carol valley.

Right
Bouillouses lake is one of the most beautiful and largest in Cerdagne.

Above
The palace of the kings of Majorca.

PERPIGNAN

Don't worry, even though Salvador Dali called its railway station the "navel of the world" and said that he felt "a kind of cosmogonic ecstasy", Perpignan does have other things to offer the visitor. A late annexation to France in 1659 as a result of the treaty of the Pyrenees, the town has not forgotten that before becoming the administrative capital of Pyrénées-Orientales, it was the capital of the kingdom of Majorca and the counts of Barcelona. It is this past which explains why "Perpinya", which is both French and Catalan – or rather Catalan and French – still looks to Barcelona rather than Montpellier or Paris.

Inside a vast polygon of boulevards which retrace the route of the old ramparts, the old town, with its lively, warm atmosphere, is reminiscent of Spain. The quarter of Saint-Jacques is particularly evocative, with its laundry hanging from the windows, chairs set up on the pavement, conversations from door to door and lively markets. Around the *place de la Loge*, the beating heart of the town, the quarter of Saint-Jean, full of tiny

Below
Venus with Necklace by Maillol, at the foot of *Loge de Mer*.

Below
The Campo Santo and the cathedral of Saint-Jean.

Above
Pénitents noirs, or black penitents,
in the Procession de la Sanch.

squares and narrow alleyways, houses some magnificent Gothic buildings, such as the maison *Xanxo* (rue de la Main-de-Fer), the *maison Julia* (rue des Fabriques-Nabot) or the *palais des Corts* (place des Orfèvres).

Its powerful walls dominate the city: the citadel is Perpignan's most spectacular monument. Built under King Louis XI, reinforced under Charles the Fifth and Philip the Second, then redesigned by Vauban, it houses the 13th- and 14th-century palace of the Kings of Majorca, whose *cour d'honneur* is a veritable masterpiece of Gothic civil architecture. The *tour de l'Hommage*, which stands before it, offers panoramic views over the city.

The cathedral of Saint-Jean is also a fine example of Southern Gothic architecture, with its rectangular façade of alternating bricks and pebbles and its unique, impressively sized nave. Its furniture includes a rare 7th-century baptismal marble font, exceptional retables and, in a side chapel, an extremely well-crafted wooden crucifix called the Devout Christ.

Among the city's other major monuments are le Castillet, the 14th-century remains of the fortifications, the *Loge de Mer*, the 15th-century, former commercial court, the 15th-century *palais de la Députation* and the 18th-century *hôtel de ville* (City Hall), the churches of Saint-Jean-leVieux (13th century) and Sainte-Marie-la-Réal (14th century) and finally the curious Campo Santo, a cloistered cemetery dating from the 14th century.

Above
The banks of the Têt
and the Castillet.

PRADES

Prades stands at the foot of Mont Canigou in a refreshing, noisy countryside full of orchards, torrents and rivers. The charm of its old quarters alone, with their wash-houses, their porches framed in pink marble and the decorated facades of the old houses, make it worth a visit. However, Prades has many other assets. Firstly, the church of Saint-Pierre, completely rebuilt in the 17th century apart from the Romanesque bell tower and housing the largest baroque retable in France. Carved by the Catalan sculptor Joseph Sunyer between 1696 and 1699, it was dedicated to Saint Peter, whose story it relates, using more than one hundred characters – statues, busts and bas-reliefs, all executed with stupendous mastery. In the rest of the church, particularly the side chapels, there is an exceptional wealth of furniture, retables, a 16th-century Christ made of buttonbush wood and an 18th-century Virgin surmounted by a gilt wood canopy. The Treasure rooms display the entire reliquary, objects made of precious metals and chalices from both the church and the abbey of Cuixà, or Cuxa. However, Prades' fame is also due to the immense personality of Pablo Casals, one of the greatest cellists in the history of music, who fled the Franco dictatorship and found refuge here in 1939. In 1950, he founded a festival of chamber music, which remains one of the foremost festivals of its type in Europe, even now that the master has passed on. Every year, between mid-July and mid-August, the best international soloists and ensembles come to Prades to perform up to twenty-five concerts in the abbey of Saint-Michel-de-Cuxa and the most beautiful churches in the region, including the church of Saint-Pierre.

Left

The statue of Saint Peter, to whom Joseph Sunyer's masterpiece is dedicated.

SAINT-MARTIN-DU-CANIGOU

This is pure emotion: faced with such a wonder, even the most hardened atheist might be converted. Perched nearly 1,100m above sea level on the edge of a precipice, the abbey, founded in the year 1,000 by Guilfred, count of Cerdagne, is, thankfully, only accessible on foot (1 hour there and back on a very steep slope), which preserves the mystical peace of the place. Destroyed in the 15th century by an earthquake, abandoned at the time of the Revolution, it was rebuilt in the 20th century. More than the church, monastic buildings and cloister, it is the incredible beauty of the site that moves visitors.

SAINT-MICHEL-DE-CUXA

There is so much peaceful grace in this valley at the foot of Le Canigou… this is a different world to that in Saint-Martin-du-Canigou – it is perhaps more ambitious and less mystical. The abbots of Saint-Michel made their sanctuary a cultural – and at times political – centre, whose influence extended throughout Catalonia. In spite of deterioration due to the Revolution and the pillaging of capitals from the Romanesque cloister – some of which are exhibited in New York – the whole abbey remains extraordinarily harmonious. Some of the most remarkable elements of this ensemble are the simple, austere church, dominated by an 11th-century square four-storey bell tower, the 11th-century crypt of the Virgin and the remains of the cloister.

Below
One of the centres of Catalan civilisation.

Top of page
The abbey of Saint-Martin-du-Canigou, or the vertigo of faith…

SALSES-LE-CHÂTEAU

One of the masterpieces of European military architecture, the fortress of Salses was built at the end of the 15th century by order of Ferdinand of Aragon, when Roussillon was still in Spanish hands. Occupying a key strategic point on the border, between the coast and the buttresses of Corbières, the fortress, with its enclosure flanked by square towers its châtelet, a 15m-wide moat, three drawbridges and an enormous keep, was long considered impregnable. The thickness of the partially embedded walls – 10m on average – rendered the artillery of the time useless. When Roussillon returned to French hands in 1659, Vauban considered razing the fortress to the ground but had to give up the idea because of the enormity of the task and so contented himself with redesigning it.

Top of page
A colossal construction considered impregnable…

Below and right
The priory gallery, with its exquisite carved décor (on the right, detail from a capital).

SERRABONE

The austerity of this priory, with its angular architecture, square bell tower and dark stone walls interspersed with rare openings, is in perfect harmony with the harsh beauty of its location, the burnt scrub, the hard-peaked mountains and the obscure ravine to which it clings. But yet, as soon as you enter, you will be amazed to discover an interior décor of unexpected refinement: an arcade supported by elegant columns, a pink marble gallery with delicately sculpted canopy and an astonishingly luminous nave. This striking contrast makes a visit to Serrabone priory unforgettable.

TAUTAVEL

Nothing seemed to point to world-wide fame for this little village. However, in 1971, 450,000-year-old human remains were found in a nearby cave called la *caune de l'Arago*. Before being dethroned by a Spaniard, Tautavel Man was long considered to be the oldest European known to man. The *Musée de la Préhistoire* uses all the most contemporary museum techniques – video, interactive terminals, dioramas, multiscreen shows, etc. – to evoke the evolution of our species and the daily life of Tautavel Man. It is fascinating.

Top of page
At the Prehistoric Museum in Tautavel…

Below
The first Europeans lived in these caves carved out of the rocky terrain.

THE YELLOW TRAIN

Between Villefranche-de-Confluent and La Tour-de-Carol runs one of the most picturesque railway tracks in France. Built between 1903 and 1927 to open up the high Catalan plains, the yellow train line meanders through superb landscapes of gorges, defiles, Mediaeval villages and castle ruins. At 18 miles per hour – sometimes speeding up to 35 mph, the maximum authorised speed – it serves 24 stations (6 compulsory stops, 18 on request), including Bolquère, which, at 1,593 metres above sea level, is the highest in France. Even now, in the time of high-speed trains, the skill required to build such a railway is staggering The figures speak for themselves: 650 structures, including nineteen tunnels and two remarkable bridges – the viaduct Séjourné and pont Gisclard – 390 curves, height difference of 1,166 metres and a record gradient of 6% – not forgetting the fact that the train uses an electrical traction system supplied by green energy from Bouillouses dam and the hydroelectric complex in the Têt valley. Suddenly, the much-maligned French railway service doesn't seem so bad...

Left page, top
The viaduct Séjourné, one of the most spectacular structures along the yellow train line.

Left page, bottom
The train station of Font-Romeu-Odeillo-Via, one of twenty-four on the 40-mile long track.

Below
Behind the ramparts, fort Libéria, built by Marshall Vauban, the most recent addition to the town's fortifications.

VILLEFRANCHE-DE-CONFLENT

This is another rare treasure. It is completely enclosed by ramparts, the oldest parts of which were built in the 11th century, in particular the amazing parapet walk designed within the thickness of the walls. The little town has been standing guard for almost a thousand years over the valleys of Têt and Cady, which lie beneath its walls. Founded in 1090 by Guillaume-Raymond, count of Cerdagne, it fell into the hands of the kings of Aragon, who reinforced its fortifications in the 14th century by flanking the walls with round towers. The omnipresent Marshal Vauban completed his predecessors' work by adding bastions and building *fort Libéria* above the town. This fort may be reached via an underground 1,000-step stairway. The town itself is laid out around two main streets – Saint-Jean and Saint-Jacques – lined with mediaeval houses with pink marble façades. The church of Saint-Jacques – curiously flanked by a Devil's tower – is remarkable for its Romanesque marble doorway and its gravestones depicting grinning death's-heads!

The main festivals in Languedoc-Roussillon

JANUARY
Limoux
Traditional carnival
(every weekend until April
and Mardi Gras)

FEBRUARY
Céret
Les Méditerranéennes, a festival
of popular music from the
Mediterranean.
Pézenas
Street festival (Mardi Gras)
Prats de Mollo
Festival of the Bear
Roquemaure
Saint Valentine's Kissing Festival

MARCH
Lunel
Camargue pony races
(until November)

APRIL
Béziers
Festival of Sainte-Aphrodise
Elne
Primavera d'Elne, a Catalan
festival and spring fair

Leucate
Mondial du Vent, a sports festival
based on the themes of wind
and sea
Marsillargues
Camargue pony races
(until end of October)
Perpignan
Procession de la Sanch
(Good Friday)
Sète
Jousting tournaments
(until end of September)

MAY - JUNE
Narbonne
Natur'ailes, a sports festival based
on the themes of wind and sea
Nîmes
Pentecost Feria
(street entertainment, bullfighting,
bodegas, etc.)

JUNE
Banyuls-sur-Mer
Fête de la Saint-Jean
(Summer Solstice
Festival)
Beaucaire
Fête du Drac, with
parades, Camargue
pony races, markets
and concerts

Bouzigues
Festival of fishermen
and Saint Peter
Le Grau-du-Roi
Vogua Monstra, festival of rowing
and Mediterranean culture
Jousting tournaments
(until end of September)
Gruissan
Festival of fishermen
and Saint Peter
Montpellier
Montpellier Dance festival,
international choreographers and
contemporary dance
Palavas-les-Flots
Jousting tournaments
(until end of September)
Perpignan
Festa Major Festival, a festival
based on the bonfires of Saint
John's Eve

DECEMBER
Narbonne
Christmas extravaganza with street entertainment, Christmas figures and Christmas market

The exact dates of the festivals vary from one year to the next. For further information, please contact the tourist boards.

JULY
Banyuls-sur-Mer
Catalan festival
Cap-d'Agde
Fête de la mer (Sea Festival)
Céret
International Sardana Festival
Feria with street shows, bullfighting, etc.
Frontignan
Fête de la mer
Limoux
International Folklore Festival in Pyrénées audoises
Mende
Mende Folklore Festival

AUGUST
Aigues-Mortes
Festival of Saint-Louis
Amélie-les-Bains
Folklore Festival
Béziers
Feria (bullfighting, bodegas, concerts, etc.)
Collioure
Feria with sea-based entertainment, bullfighting, etc.
Mont-Louis
Festival of Saint-Louis, with historical re-enactments

Montpellier
Fête de la Saint-Roch, with religious ceremonies, conferences, entertainment and shows
Pérols
Herdsmens' Mass in the arenas, with herdsmen and *Arlésiennes*
Prades
Festival Pablo Casals (chamber music)
Rivesaltes
Carnaval du Babeau, with entertainment and mediaeval market
Sète
Festival of Saint-Louis, with street entertainment and jousting tournaments

SEPTEMBER
Nîmes
Féria des Vendanges (wine harvest festival)

OCTOBER
Banyuls-sur-Mer
Fête des Vendanges (wine harvest festival)

AUDE
Tourist board, rue Moulin-de-la-Seigne, 11000 Carcassonne, France.
Tel. +33 (0)4 68 11 66 01.

GARD
Tourist board, 3 place des Arènes, 30011 Nîmes Cedex, France.
Tel. +33 (0)4 66 36 96 30.

HÉRAULT
Tourist board, avenue des Moulins, 34034 Montpellier Cedex, France.
Tel. +33 (0)4 67 67 71 71.

LOZÈRE
Tourist board, 14 boulevard Henri-Bourrillon,
48002 Mende Cedex, France.
Tel. +33 (0)4 66 65 60 00.

PYRÉNÉES-ORIENTALES
Tourist board, quai De-Lattre-de-Tassigny, 66005 Perpignan Cedex, France.
Tel. +33 (0)4 68 34 29 94.

Contents

Aude • 5
Alet-les-Bains • 6
Bages and Sigean • 6
Carcassonne • 8
Castelnaudary and
    the abbey of Saint-Papoul • 10
Fontfroide • 12
Gruissan • 14
La Clape • 15
Lagrasse • 16
Limoux • 17
Narbonne • 18
Natural regional park
    of Narbonnaise
    en Méditerranéee • 20
Port-la-Nouvelle • 22
Rennes-le-Château • 23
Cathar castles in
    the Aude region • 24

Hérault • 53
Agde • 54
Ambrussum • 57
Béziers • 58
Clermont-l'Hérault • 62
Ensérune • 63
Lake Thau • 64
Frontignan • 65
La Grande-Motte • 66
Lodève • 67
Minerve and Minervois • 68
Montpellier • 70
Navacelles • 74
Olargues • 75

Gard • 31
Aigues-Mortes • 32
Alès • 33
Anduze • 34
Beaucaire • 35
La Camargue gardoise • 36
Nîmes • 38
Pont-Saint-Esprit • 43
The Pont du Gard • 44
Saint-Gilles • 46
Saint-Roman • 46
Sommières • 47
Uzès • 48
Valbonne (Charterhouse of) • 50
Villeneuve-lès-Avignon • 51

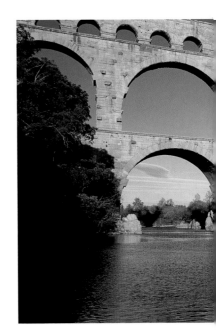

From Palavas-les-Flots
   to Maguelone • **76**
Natural regional park of Haut-
   Languedoc • **78**
Pézenas • **82**
Saint-Bauzille-de-Putois
   et la grotte des Demoiselles • **84**
Saint-Guilhem-le-Désert • **84**
Saint-Pons-de-Thomières • **86**
Salvetat-sur-Agout • **88**
Sète • **89**
The Via Domitia • **92**
Across Aude and Hérault:
   the canal du Midi • **94**

La Lozère • 97
Aubrac • **98**
The Causses • **103**
The Cévennes coast road • **106**
The Gorges du Tarn and gorges
   de la Jonte • **108**
Mende • **110**
Marvejols • **112**
Mont Aigoual and Mont Lozère • **113**
Pont-de-Montvert • **116**
Villefort and its lake • **117**

Pyrénées-Orientales • 121
Le Canigou • **122**
Castelnou • **123**
Collioure • **124**
Elne • **125**
Eus • **125**

Font-Romeu and La Cerdagne • **126**
Galamus (gorges and hermitage)
   • **127**
Ille-sur-Têt • **128**
Mont-Louis • **129**
The natural regional park of
   Pyrénées catalanes • **130**
Perpignan • **132**
Prades • **134**
Saint-Martin-du-Canigou • **135**
Saint-Michel-de-Cuxa • **135**
Salses-le-Château • **136**
Serrabone • **136**
Tautavel • **137**
The Yellow Train • **138**
Villefranche-de-Conflent • **139**

**The main festivals in
Languedoc-Roussillon** • 140

Bibliography

Le Canal du Midi, René Gast and Bruno Barbier, Editions Ouest-France

Le Languedoc-Roussillon, Simonetta Greggio and Richard Nourry, Editions Ouest-France

La Route des abbayes en Languedoc-Roussillon, Frédérique Barbut, Catherine Bibollet and Richard Nourry, Editions Ouest-France

Saint-Guilhem-le-Désert, Frédérique Barbut and Richard Nourry, Editions Ouest-France

Carcassonne, Jean-Pierre Panouillé, Editions Ouest-France

Montpellier et ses environs, Yvon Busson, Editions Ouest-France

Comprendre la tragédie des Cathares, Claude Lebédel and Catherine Bibollet, Editions Ouest-France

Acknowledgements

The authors would like to thank Patricia de Pouzilhac
and Dominique Klépandy of the Regional Tourist Board of Languedoc-Roussillon.

Editor: Henri Bancaud

Editorial Coordination: Solenne Lambert

Layout and photoengraving: Nord Compo, Villeneuve d'Ascq (59)

Printing: Pollina, Luçon (85) - L58960A